WEIRD CANADIAN WEATHER

Catastrophes, Ice Storms, Floods, Tornadoes, Hurricanes and Tsunamis

A.H. Jackson

BLUE
BIKE
BOOKS

The Publisher: Blue Bike Books
Website: www.bluebikebooks.com

Library and Archives Canada Cataloguing in Publication

Jackson, A.H., 1944–
    Weird Canadian weather / by A.H. Jackson.

ISBN 978-1-897278-39-0

    1. Canada—Climate—Miscellanea. 2. Weather—Miscellanea.
I. Title.

QC985.J32 2009   551.6571   C2008-907955-8

Project Director: Nicholle Carrière
Project Editor: Kathy van Denderen
Production: HR Media
Illustrations: Peter Tyler, Roger Garcia, Patrick Hénaff, Roly Wood
Cover Image: Courtesy of Dreamstime; © Alysta | Dreamstime.com

We acknowledge the support of the Alberta Foundation for the Arts for our publishing program.

We acknowledge the financial support of the Government of Canada through the Book Publishing Industry Development Program (BPIDP) for our publishing activities.

Canadian Patrimoine
Heritage canadien

PC: 1

DEDICATION

For my wife Maria, a fountain of inspiration and patience.

–A.H. Jackson

ACKNOWLEDGEMENTS

Commercial pilots know inclement weather is dangerous and fly their aircraft to great heights to avoid atmospheric problems. They cruise in the stratosphere and get a bird's-eye view of happenings on our planet's surface. These pilots report significant weather formations, volcanic eruptions, cyclonic cloud movement and a host of other meteorological problems that assist in weather forecasting. From me, they get special thanks for information compiled in this book.

Another thanks goes to Environment Canada and their marvellous cornucopia of online information, as almost anything you need to know about weather is there and kept current. Big thanks to *Wikipedia*, the online encyclopedia, where everything I used to know and forgot is there for the reminding. I also want to thank the media doomsayers, the Moses people, for making me want to write this book. Doomsayers have spouted end-of-the-world dogma for centuries, but always part time and through placards, leaflets and street-corner oration. That changed during the early '60s, when scientists revealed the unhealthy side of smoking. Did people quit? No, they simply filed the evidence into their subconscious minds and carried on smoking. But the joie de vivre had gone, and every puff now included a nagging, subconscious concern for their health. Canada became a nation of school kids smoking behind the barn and a kind of collective guilt opened the doors for the Moses people. No more placards, leaflets or spouting dogma from street corners, because now they had the national guilt, a gold mine.

Guilt begets guilt, and as Canada entered the new millennium, the national guilt encompassed everything from baby seals to Alberta cacti. Saving the country had become big business and the agendas legion. Arctic ice melting, cute baby seals, save the animals, fish stocks depleting, not enough electricity, trees dying, and on and on—and it's all our fault. Do I feel guilty? No, and neither should you, because all of these ills are symptoms of global overpopulation, a terminal disease almost completely ignored by doomsayers and politicians alike. Fixing the symptoms is ludicrous, as is enabling the disease by providing food and monetary aid to countries with unchecked populations. Food and money simply stoke the fires of overpopulation and increase global pollution. Canadian aid dollars could be better spent constructing schools and prophylactic factories. Okay, enough rant—anymore and I'd be sounding like a Moses man myself.

Big thanks to those sunshine folks at Blue Bike Books for aiding and abetting in my belief that Canadian weather was, is and will always be weird.

CONTENTS

INTRODUCTION

*Take precautions, pilgrim; thy way is fraught
with danger.*

Weather is the voice of our planet; it rumbles, crashes, zaps and smells like ozone. It is all there in an easy-to-understand sign language that surely provided the impetus for human speech. A few zaps, a couple of fried cavemen and the hairy survivors would have learned to interpret weather rather quickly. They fashioned tools, so not much of a jump to a guttural warning not to follow the monkeys up a tree during storms. A crack of thunder and their simian relatives would scamper up the tallest trees and hang from branches like tiny lightning rods. Thunder was the primal scare, the huge fear factor of storms, so the first spoken word was probably a loud imitation accompanied by a wagging finger. That conscious decision to head for ground and not follow the monkeys contributed hugely to human evolution. Little wonder they're called cavemen—only one word and the trees were full of crispy critters.

Canadians are brighter now, and there are fewer trees, but weather is still a fear factor and the Big Kahuna of human stupidity. A thousand centuries go by and extreme weather still finds Canadians heading for the trees like monkeys. Why? Because like those ancient simians, they think bad things happen to other people and ignore the signs of imminent danger: black clouds, driving rain, hail, lightning, thunder, whirring noises, ears popping, the smell of ozone, and on and on, which all mean the same now as in the beginning. Get to your cave, man.

Having learned early in life to read weather signs and having narrowly missed the fate of the monkey on numerous occasions, I decided to write this book as a kind of weather primer for the uninitiated and a historical oversight of extreme and weird Canadian weather. Am I qualified? Imminently—I have been in conflict with weather so many times that it's made me an anticipator of its weird and wonderful ways.

A little background music, maestro—some Richard Wagner, please.

Now visualize a small boy (*moi* at seven years old) riding his brand-new bike into a thunderstorm. Dad had run out of mix for an impromptu party, and I was on a mission to replenish the stock.

"Looking real bad outside, Dad."

"It's only a five-minute ride, son. Wear your new raincoat."

Thunder crackled, lightning slashed the night sky, and I, wearing my new yellow slicker, peddled furiously across the neighbour's lawn in driving rain. It was a shortcut to the store taken many times, but on that night I had to watch for the new clothesline, a wire used to run our neighbour's dog. Anticipating that wire, I ducked my head and found myself at ground zero of an immense explosion. Lightning had struck one of the tall pines used to secure the dog wire and blown up both trees. Caught in the middle and knocked flat, I endured a seemingly endless avalanche of steaming kindling. A few moments later, I crawled from the pile, checked my bike for damage, and finding none, resumed my journey. Not until I reached the store did I find that the hood of my new yellow slicker had completely melted away.

A narrow escape, but the next year, in early spring, I was standing on a Lake Erie beach watching an amazing spectacle and hoping it would come closer. A waterspout, and like it read my mind, that water twister suddenly turned and sizzled for shore like a tango dancer. It was hot, no wind, hard to breathe, and the whirling apparition had almost reached land. Not until I heard a noise like an oncoming freight train did I realize the danger. In a panic, I turned and ran for the cottonwood trees. Behind me, the spout dropped its tango act and tore into those trees like a buzz saw. Only dumb luck saved me. I fell into a ditch and stayed there until the tornado moved back to water.

The next year featured another close shave, a bigger wind this time—a hurricane they called Hazel. As I rode my bike home from school, I saw the storm-warning signs: flat light and low, greenish-grey clouds. Only something looked wrong with the picture. I got off my bike, put my back to the wind, and pointed my left arm at the approaching weather front—a trick I learned from studying pilot's meteorology. A front coming from the west, but the radio weather report had the hurricane approaching from the south. If that western front was cold and should meet the hurricane, there would be hell to pay. Only the radio report had said the hurricane was dissipating and promised only sporadic rainfall, so I turned monkey and forgot about the signs.

The next morning, I rode my bike to school in a light rain that got progressively heavier as the day wore on. When the finish bell rang, the weatherman's promised sporadic rain had become a deluge and turned roads into rivers. I could not get home and sought refuge at a schoolmate's house. My friend's mother called my parents, and they decided I should remain there for the night. We watched television until the screen went black. No problem; the storm outside looked more interesting, and we watched out a window until a flying rose trellis smashed through it, turning the living room into a battlefield.

But through all the excitement of bailing water and boarding up the window, I knew something even more dangerous was on the prowl. Although it was too dark to see, I could still read the signs: a strange but familiar freight-train noise louder than Hazel's wind and explosions of light coming down the street. Power transformers atop poles were exploding, and I, figuring that Hazel had spawned a tornado, quickly hustled my hosts to their basement. Once again, I was lucky—the tornado moved off in a different direction, and the awful train noise became just the howl of Hazel and the drumming of hard rain.

Another close shave, and it left behind a resolve in me to learn more about extreme weather. At 14, I soloed an airplane and got to examine clouds close up; at 16, lightning struck the hood of my first car; and when I was 18, it struck a nearby golf cart, killing the two occupants. Now a young man, I had become aware of my affinity with nature's extreme side. At 31 years old, and having survived other atmospheric assaults, I found myself driving a C-130 airplane for Dick Aviation and ferrying supplies for U.S. troops in Vietnam. That adventure lasted only three months, but it served up every type of extreme weather imaginable, and some…unimaginable.

Climate Change

Is Canada's climate changing? Sure, our world is constantly in flux. Continents move, volcanoes erupt, wildfires burn, ocean currents change direction, and solar flares and sunspots cause all sorts of problems. Since the earth formed, no two days have seen the same weather.

EVERYONE'S TALKING

Climate Conundrums

If, indeed, climate change is accelerating as the media people say it is, how bad is it? That depends on your perspective; in 1970, a hurricane killed 300,000 people in Bangladesh, and I bet survivors thought that was climate change. Had you been around for the Dirty Thirties, you would have witnessed the scouring of American and Canadian prairie lands by drought and winds. The great Dust Bowl devastated parts of Canada for 10 years and was thought to be climate change. Go back a few thousand years, and you'd be up to your tush in ice. The last great Ice Age (the Quaternary) petered out only 10,000 years ago, just a millisecond on the historical clock. That icy time began two million years ago and featured glacial (cold) periods interspersed with interglacial (warm) periods. Gone, but still ticking faintly, the Quaternary spawned a last-gasp cold period during the 13th century called the Little Ice Age that accounted for unpredictable weather right up to the 19th century. Glaciers advanced, winter hung around until

June, and the harvest of summer crops couldn't be counted upon to feed the population.

In Canada at the start of the 17th century, ice covered Lake Superior until June and glaciers were advancing, and by the year 1650, glaciers had advanced worldwide, and people were thinking it could not get any worse. Only it did. All over Europe, canals and harbours froze solid during winters, and the summer months were cold and miserable. During the winter of 1780, New York's harbour froze solid, and in the winter of 1812, the St. Lawrence River could be crossed on foot and was garrisoned by British soldiers who feared an American invasion of Québec. That is climate change, and what caused such a dramatic jerk in a usually gentle cycle of warm and cold? Scientists are not exactly sure, but they suspect a change in cyclical sunspot activity, along with a few home-grown helpers.

Evidence from deep-sea drilling points to volcanic dust and gasses as being the helpers. We know both cause climate change, and it is feasible that large eruptions changed the atmospheric chemistry and combined with a decrease in sunspot activity to act as a catalyst for an icy Quaternary mini-episode. Moreover, we have not seen the last of the Quaternary; we're still hanging onto its coattails and are presently experiencing an interglacial period that could last hundreds of years. Warming melts ice, that is a fact, but according to the media doomsayers, the world's weather is the worst ever, and it's our fault. Not true, because global weather mortality is way down, and while some places get stomped on, others enjoy boom times. It has always been that way. In Canada, extreme weather causes flooding of the Red River and millions of dollars in damages, while farther south, that same rainfall tops up Arizona's water-depleted Lake Powell, and tourist operations are at full bore again. One door closes and another opens; it is nature's way.

Are we to blame? Are we polluting the world to climate change? Sure, our world is overpopulated, overurbanized, insanely industrialized and careless with toxic wastes. Only the world doesn't need our help; it can pollute itself, no problem. Pine trees sweat volatile chemicals into the atmosphere, forest fires send up noxious gasses, volcanoes are constantly erupting, desert winds loft sand, and ocean waves fling up so much salt it can sometimes be tasted in the air.

An overly enthusiastic belch of particulates from a large volcano can produce frigid weather in July and cause crops to fail. These are called volcanic winters, and a few deserve mention. One such eruption, in 536 AD, blocked sunlight in the Northern Hemisphere for over a year and probably caused the infamous period in world history known as the Dark Ages, when crops shrivelled, people starved and disease killed one-quarter of the world's population. In 1815, Indonesia's Mt. Tambora exploded, sending so much topography into the atmosphere that it caused North America's Year Without Summer, when crop failure forced a mass migration westward. In that same area of Indonesia, in the Sunda Straits, a volcano called Krakatoa went on behaving like an infected tooth for over a century until 1883, when it disintegrated in the ultimate big bang, or what volcanologists call an ultra-Plinian eruption, sending ash 20 kilometres into the air and affecting global weather for years. Now that was climate change, but it still pales when compared to the great Chinese flood of 1887, when after weeks of unrelenting rain, the Yellow River overflowed, drowning one million people. Millions more died in the aftermath, of starvation, disease and despair.

Floods are catastrophic events, but without them we probably wouldn't be here; hard rain erodes fertile soil that over-burdened rivers deposit in areas unsuitable for raising crops. The ancient Egyptians depended on the annual Nile flood for their very existence. Most thought it a gift from their gods, but a few savvy priests knew that rain in faraway lands caused the Nile to rise, and they instituted a rudimentary weather service. Travellers brought weather news, and priests kept records and predicted the river's rise and fall.

Venetian traders employed a similar record-collecting system. Since weather sank ships, the Venetians made sure their captains received a basic education in meteorology. Each morning, the captain would stand on his ship's foredeck to experience the coming day. Wind direction, smell, feel, cloud shapes and feeling the cloth were important since sea travel in those days consisted of daylight dashes from port to port in vessels unable to weather any storm.

What was "feeling the cloth"? That was simply stroking a cloth soaked in salt-brine and allowed to dry. When humidity increased, the cloth would soak up moisture and feel damp—a rudimentary hydrometer that was used by sea captains for centuries.

Both systems were historical bright lights that, given time, might have matured into a weather service and saved count-less lives. Only time ran out, and the world reverted to deal-ing with whatever came along and had to wait centuries for Samuel Morse's telegraph key. The first telegraph message transmitted in Canada went from Toronto to Hamilton on December 19, 1846, and was probably a weather report.

In 1871, the Canadian government established a meteoro-logical service, and by the 1880s, Canada had transcontinental rail and telegraph lines across the country, and weather warnings and probabilities were disseminated to interested parties. Grain farmers got warned of impending storms by large, coloured balls on the sides of freight cars, while ship captains and fishermen consulted their local telegraph-equipped lighthouse keeper.

Then along came Dr. Bell with his telephone, and weather information fairly exploded across the nation via newspapers. If a city or town experienced a violent thunderstorm, the editor would simply pick up the phone and alert newspapers down the line. People in rural areas, with no access to a daily newspaper, could simply call the local telephone exchange and get a weather report. It was a bright idea, soon dimmed by World War I, but destined to burn brighter with the advent of post-war air travel.

Pilots needed up-to-date weather forecasts, and in 1932, the University of Toronto offered a masters degree in meteor-ological studies. Smart people were soon making semi-accurate predictions, and as the years progressed, they got even more accurate. But oftentimes they would get it completely wrong, and that could be devastating—going to bed expecting to wake up to sporadic rainfall but finding a hurricane instead can be traumatic for sailors, farmers and schoolboys alike.

Weather reports are useful tools; use them, but do not forget your instincts. If the weather does not feel, smell or look right, it probably isn't. Better take the umbrella, and when incessant talk of climate change and global warming gets you down, just remember the year 1815, the infamous Year Without Summer, when a volcanic eruption caused winter in July and inspired a massive migration. Or consider the Great Blizzard of 1899, when the American state of Florida experienced statewide blizzard conditions for the first and only time in its history.

There is nothing new under the sun; weird weather happening now has happened before and will happen again. But even weird weather needs perspective. How does our sense of weird stack up to, let's say...deep space, where radio astronomers recently found acetic acid (that's right, vinegar) in a huge cloud of gasses called Sagittarius B2 North? And not to be outdone on the weirdness scale, British astronomers recently identified a cloud composed mostly of alcohol, enough to fill half a billion swimming pools. Now that is...weird.

CONTRIBUTORS TO CLIMATE CHANGE

Cause and Effect

How we treat our planet affects weather; that old adage, "You reap what you sow," is on the button but old-fashioned. A more modern version should read, "What you reap may come back to haunt you." Civilization has reaped a lot: 15 million square kilometres plowed up for farmland, 10 million square kilometres of forest cut down and 32 square kilometres for live-stock grazing. That only leaves 90 million square kilometres, and loggers are attacking that vigorously. Deforestation is progressing so rapidly that just to keep pace with loss and allow for slow regeneration, 250 million trees would have to be planted every year—and we should be doing that because trees use carbon dioxide and modify temperature extremes. Trees also keep soil from eroding, and we need that, because every year, around 75 million tons of precious topsoil is blown away by winds or eroded by rainwater. In 1776, the average depth of topsoil on U.S. and Canadian prairie lands was 22 centimetres, a mean depth that over the years has diminished to just less than 15 centimetres. Not good, and it's worse in some undeveloped countries with unfettered population growth, where soil depth is half what it was a century ago. A grim future may await those nations as sometime down the road their growing populations may experience starvation on a massive scale.

A good number of those conditions the media Moses people call "contributors to global climate change" are actually symptoms of a planet made sick by overpopulation. Stripping the planet of protective forests and groundcover causes greenhouse gas emissions to rise, even without burning fossil fuels. Magazines used to have great full-page cartoons, and the one I remember best featured two Martians approaching Earth in a flying saucer: one had a horrified look on its face and said, "Don't land! That planet is infected with people."

Our planet is infected; it's sick and getting sicker, and no amount of rules and laws is going to help unless overpopulation is addressed and not swept under carpets by politicians frightened of hot-potato issues.

Overpopulation is a global catastrophe waiting to happen and will occur the moment *just in time* food distribution fails. "Just in time" is a Japanese concept for streamlining industrial output. Most manufacturing companies no longer warehouse components needed to build their products and have them delivered at the exact point in production when needed— just in time. That is how produce arrives in the cities of developed countries, just in time for Martha's trip to the market. Looking for a good scare? Do what I did and find out how much grub is in your city. Toronto would last a week in the face of disaster: supermarket shelves cleared in one day, home supplies gone in six or seven, and millions of people

Hey, Martha! This writer guy is scaring me. What the heck is "just in time" food distribution?

would go hungry. Toronto doesn't need a cataclysmic weather disaster for that to happen; a trucker's strike would do the trick...a dangerous situation.

When I was growing up, the Great Depression was still fresh in people's minds, and everyone had a pantry. My mother kept one filled with cases of canned salmon, mushroom soup and peas—chipped salmon on toast—yuck! But if the need ever arose, she could make enough of her Depression dinners to last us months.

Not much fun, but worse for undeveloped countries because *all* their food arrives just in time. By the year 2050, the world's population will have doubled, and food production will be a tenuous affair, as any cataclysmic weather disaster will have people in undeveloped, or semi-developed, countries starving when the daily bag of rice or lentils runs out.

Human infection is also exhausting our planet of its natural ability to control latent heat.

Our world is in a temporary warming phase, and cutting down heat-reflecting forests for building materials and charcoal is inviting disaster. A global warming trend causes stronger updrafts at the equator that push air farther north, depriving temperate zones of almost any moisture. Desert areas are already growing in size, and large ones like the Sahara are growing almost one percent a year and reflect enormous amounts of heat. More heat creates bigger deserts, which in turn reflect more heat. It's a conundrum, and the timing couldn't be worse. We need those forests, but all we are doing to protect them is talking carbon tax and buying dumb light bulbs.

I'm reminded of what occurred on a tiny island in a remote corner of the South Pacific, an island once known as Pleasant Island. Now called Nauru, that island had one commodity the world needed—phosphate rock, a fertilizer composed of marine organisms, bird droppings and coral. For that, its 2000 residents saw their entire island mined almost to extinction by foreign companies. However, that's not where the analogy lies. In 1998, that island secured independence, and instead of stopping the extinction, they imported workers, increased production and mined the island to death. The fertilizer ran out, and the island's irresponsible residents were forced to share a narrow strip of beach with their workers and import all their food supplies. But those Naurunians hadn't been sitting on their hands while their island became lifeless desert; they talked a lot—they talked about a reclamation tax and how to repair the damage. In the end, they did nothing except buy light bulbs and look for a new island.

Nauru is a micro-shot of the same cannibalistic process occurring around the globe today. Too many people wanting too much from an already exhausted planet could be the end, and like the Naurunians, we may have to look for another island.

Hey, Martha! Doom boy has us moving to another planet. Is that possible?

Yes, more than possible. Migration is a natural human response—when things get tough, people move to better places. But we're out of places, and the only way out, is out—out there among the stars and light years away. How could we possibly get there?

Sadly, overpopulation does have one solitary benefit—an increased opportunity for genius. Genius is like cream, it rises to the top, but you need a lot of milk to get some. We have a lot of people, and will soon have lots more, so chances are good that a genius will come along and find us a quick way to the Promised Land.

Sounds iffy, and it will be if we don't stop addressing the planet's symptoms instead of the illness. Talking carbon tax and buying light bulbs while our planet is chewed to death by overpopulation is like shooting elephants with a BB gun.

What we need are massive birth control programs, forest and pastureland reclamation, polluters thrown into prisons, stopping the slaughter of marine life, changing the diets of entire populations, and a general clean up of this mess once called Eden. The Bible got it wrong; God never threw us out of Eden—he left us in charge. God's gardeners, and we're totally responsible for fixing the screw-ups. It's another Job test, and if we don't stop turning God's beloved whales and trees into sushi and charcoal, infinite patience will run out and turn us into pillars of salt.

But on the bright side, our planet is still fixable, and God has supplied the tools…our brains. We simply have to use them, and do a lot more than talk and buy light bulbs.

Hey, Martha! I wonder why this writer guy is down on eco-friendly light bulbs?

Only CFL bulbs are at issue here, and for three reasons: compact fluorescent lights, or CFLs, contain mercury, a dangerous neurotoxin; fluorescent lighting is old-hat technology already supplanted by LED (light-emitting diode) and plasma bulbs; and it's an ecology mafia power tester. If Big Business can make the world use CFL light bulbs, it can get away with anything.

Need some convincing?

Here is what you are supposed to do if a CFL light bulb breaks:

Shut off all air conditioners or heaters to keep them from circulating mercury vapour. Open windows and doors to air out the place. Pregnant women and small children should leave the room while the contaminated area is cleaned by a professional remediation service, or by someone you don't particularly care for wearing a dust mask and gloves.

In the United States, the Department of Environmental Protection has issued a warning that CFLs not be used in children's bedrooms or playrooms.

Worse is throwing these things in the trash and allowing even more mercury to seep into the environment from landfills—an already huge problem caused by people tossing away long fluorescent bulbs. Acid rain is bad, but mercury rain is much worse and is already exceeding acceptable Environmental Protection Agency limits in 12 U.S. states.

Using these bulbs is both dangerous and dumb as fluorescent technology is already being replaced by safe LED or plasma bulbs—both of which provide superior light and use less power than CFLs. There's no logical reason for using these things, except…

Muscle flexing by the eco-mafia, pure and simple. Ecology is big business, and convincing governments to make using CFL light bulbs mandatory is a short road to riches. It's a global money grab, and you thought "green" meant eco-friendly.

Anyway, that's my take on CFL bulbs, and while you may not agree, please do not use those bulbs around children or pets.

Weather: The Nuts and Bolts

Our sun makes weather. Earth is round, and the curvature deflects solar radiation, except at the equator, which bakes in direct radiation. The equatorial oceans heat up, water evaporates, rises, cools, and falls as rain in a relentless cycle. Earth's atmosphere is an extension of those oceans; they feed and propel it, make it calm and angry and govern temperatures.

Our atmosphere is a vast ocean, with currents, variable depths, density and weight. Being "light as air" is a misnomer, as the breathing stuff weighs in at one kilogram per square centimetre—that's one ton pressing down on every square foot. It's not called "the column" for nothing, and little wonder we have joint problems and walk on two feet. Pity the four-legged animals; being big and swaybacked is no fun, so stop overfeeding the dog.

WEATHER VS. CLIMATE

You Can't Have One without the Other

What is the difference between weather and climate? Weather is simply a disruption of the long-term expectation of what we call the climate. British Columbia residents, for example, expect warm, dry summers with only the odd arctic cold snap in winter—that's climate. But if they get a weeklong downpour in July, that's weather, foul weather. During the summer of 1955, the city of Montréal saw 33 days of temperatures above 30°C, and many residents believed their weather had become climate and blamed American atom bomb testing.

Weather and climate are two distinct fields of study; meteorologists concern themselves with weather occurring now, while climatologists work with relics of past events: tree rings, sediment cores from ocean bottoms, glaciers, pollen trapped in ice, amber and sedimentary strata in rocks. While divergent in studies, both these schools work towards the same goal: a better understanding of weather events.

The Highs and Lows

Warm air holds water vapour and rises. Because it rises, its weight is reduced, and therefore some of the column of mercury in a barometer falls back into the reservoir bulb indicating the arrival of a low-pressure area. Cold air is dry and dense. Its weight pushes mercury up the barometer column to indicate high pressure. Low pressure usually indicates bad weather, while highs are associated with sunshine and fair weather. Low-pressure cells rise when encountering areas of high pressure, and at cooler altitudes, the low-pressure cells lose water vapour—it rains, it pours, and it can sometimes get downright nasty.

Big lows crossing the breadth of North America are called cyclonic storm systems because they pinwheel counter-clockwise because of the earth's rotation (known as the Coriolis effect). Cyclonic storms can bring along all manner of nasty weather, including tornadoes. That's bad, but without rain, our crops would dry up, so we endure the odd cranky storm cell and hope it will go away quickly. When it does, the sky turns blue, and we're out walking the dog in warm sunshine and enjoying the high.

Canada gets many highs, and most originate from the lati-tudes 30 to 35 degrees north and south, the so-called horse latitudes. The horse latitudes are the birthing ground of Canada's high-pressure maritime weather cells. This area lies under the subtropical ridge, a global belt of high pressure caused by falling, vapour-exhausted equatorial air—hot air rises, cools at altitude and releases all its water in the form of rain. Bone dry, this cool air falls onto the ocean's surface and gently moves off in a northeasterly direction to form trade winds, the prevailing pattern of easterly flowing tropical air and the perfect place for old-time sailing ships. But pity those ships that blundered into the downfall, because con-stant high pressure causes flat seas with little or no wind, an atmospheric trap for sailing ships that required wind to sail. At times, those ships would stay becalmed for weeks, a situation some historians believe earned this calm weather belt its name. Rumour had it that ships carrying horses and running short of animal fodder tossed half the horses over-board to save the remaining animals. The story is probably not true—the name most certainly came from the slang words "dead horse money," meaning the monies advanced to sailors before a ship sailed—an advance worked off over the length of the voyage, which in the horse latitudes could be a long time.

Aside from affording calm winds and seas, horse latitudes are dry as toast and mostly responsible for the world's temperate zones, the great deserts such as Sahara, Kalahari and the U.S. southwest. But the horse latitudes send mainly pleasant weather to Canada, unless they are bullied northward by something big and mean.

Meet the Niños—The Ultimate Lows

El Niño (little boy) is the Big Kahuna of low pressure, a real killing machine. This monster appears every few years in the Pacific because, for inexplicable reasons, the usually constant trade winds slow or stop, and the seas go flat as pancakes and absorb massive amounts of sunlight. Now energized, a dripping monster as big as Prince Edward Island rears up and moves

along the equator towards the eastern Pacific, forcing high-pressure air westward. Indonesia will have sunshine instead of monsoon and will experience drought and famine, while in the east, the monster's extreme low pressure causes heavy rains to fall on the Peruvian desert and massive floods ensue. The monster can sit for months producing patterns of high and low pressure that affect weather far from the equatorial Pacific. This results in higher temperatures in western Canada and the upper plains of the United States, colder temperatures in the southern United States and drought on the east coast of southern Africa. Higher temperatures in western Canada push unstable air towards the east in huge cells that collide with continental air and cause all manner of nastiness: thunderstorms, hail, tornadoes, heat waves and unseasonable cool temps should they happen to drag down some arctic air.

El Niño is all-powerful but can sometimes get a little confused. In 1994, El Niño spawned a monster hurricane called John that wandered around for a record 31 days. A Class 5 blow, Big John first went into the eastern Pacific to give everybody a scare, then without making landfall, it reversed course and travelled all the way to the western Pacific to give the Indonesians a fright. A few days later it inexplicably reversed and backtracked to where it originated, a total distance of 13,000 kilometres. Since John travelled in both the eastern and western Pacific, it earned a duel designation: hurricane and typhoon. Confused maybe, but had the sea been slightly warmer to the north, Big John might well have gotten unconfused and visited Canada for a couple of weeks.

Even a confused El Niño can be a boon for Canadians. A summertime equatorial event will drive warm water north, and the following marine life can be a bonanza for hard-pressed West Coast fishermen. During a winter event, El Niño tends to warm the air over much of Canada, especially in wheat-growing Manitoba and Saskatchewan. Great for fishermen and farmers, but not so good for British Columbia ski resort operators, as snowfall is considerably reduced in that province.

El Niño has a little sister, La Niña (little girl), who does the exact opposite of her big brother; she speeds up the trade winds, building huge waves that cool equatorial oceans and disrupting the normal flow of high-altitude jet streams. This disruption can play havoc with normal Canadian weather patterns; in 2007, La Niña subjected Canadians to fierce snowstorms and the coldest winter in years. Those storms left our Arctic covered with almost two metres of fresh snow, and for a time had media doomsayers talking about global cooling. La Niña is bad for Canadian fishermen, farmers and media doomsayers, but British Columbia ski resort operators anticipate her visits with a macabre relish.

Air moves, it heats, cools and flows like an ocean current until it meets resistance and eddies into pools called warm or cold cells. The leading edges of these cells, or fronts, can be relied upon for some kind of action. Cold air usually moves from west to east, and the front may feature narrow bands of thunderstorms and severe winds. Warm air generally moves in a northeasterly direction, preceded by fog and light rain. Warm air is slower, and being less dense because of higher temperatures, will climb a mass of cooler air and form a slope characterized by uplifting altocumulus clouds. Heavy rain and surprises can be expected from both sides of an elevated warm front. When fronts have passed over, a complete cloud cover indicates a warm air mass, while sunshine and blue skies indicate cold. Which is worse? Both can be bad. Warm air is less dense and can be wedged higher by faster moving cold fronts. Higher altitudes mean cooler temperatures and storms, while inversely, a warm front encountering a slow or stuck-in-place (occluded) cold air will move higher and horizontally and cause a similar and sometimes worse reaction. Be wary of warm, low-pressure cells; they can spawn violent storms and tornadoes—better buy a barometer.

In the past, every rural Canadian who could afford the cost owned a barometer. Canadian grain farmers depended on them, and those unable to afford one used a teakettle. The farmer's wife kept a kettle filled to the top of the spout, and an overflow meant high pressure and hubby better get to his plow. The barometer-owning prairie farmer would rise up in the morning, tap the instrument, and walk outside to emulate Venetian sea captains. He sniffed the air, observed the clouds and held a wet finger into the wind. That done, he would walk back inside to announce his daily prediction to the family.

Hey, Martha! Mercury is fallin'. There's gonna be a blow. I'll do the plowing tomorrow.

Martha's husband was mostly right, but even when wrong, he enjoyed a holiday. Farmers without barometers and weather-savvy wives took whatever came along, and many suffered the crispy consequence. Caught plowing in a thunderstorm was no fun, because both farmer and horses were the tallest objects for miles around.

Sunlight

Contrary to popular thought, and even though they are called solar rays, sunshine does not arrive on earth as rays or beams. Sunlight strikes the earth in three distinct photon particle packets: short ultraviolet photons, and two packets about equal in size, the visible and infrared. Ultraviolet photons are mostly dissipated by ozone in the upper atmosphere, and since these particles are detrimental to eyes and skin, it's a bad idea to allow ozone-depleting chemicals into the atmosphere. Visible solar particles, the ones we use for vision, and plants utilize for photosynthesis, are responsible for about half the world's heating, while infrared photons, the ones that make sunshine feel warm, are responsible for the other half.

Only about half the sunlight reaching our planet is retained by land and seas; the other half is either reflected back into space or absorbed by the different levels of our atmosphere. But even the earth-retained half is reflected out as thermal radiation when rocks and seas cool. If this did not happen, our planet would become as hot as the sun, and for the earth to maintain a stable, life-supporting temperature, what reflects must equal what is absorbed. When this balance gets out of whack, an enhanced greenhouse effect occurs.

Hey, Martha! Greenhouse effect—isn't that what that nature guy on TV says is overheating the planet?

Greenhouse Effect

Many media people talk about it, and it's getting a bad rap.
We need the greenhouse effect; without it, the average temperature of our planet would be around −18°C instead of 14°C.

What is the greenhouse effect? Simply put, certain gasses
found in our troposphere (the zone of atmosphere closest to
the earth) contain molecules that absorb and react to earth-
reflected infrared light—they absorb this light, get excited,
heat up and radiate heat back to earth. The most plentiful
of these reactive gasses are water vapour (95 percent), carbon
dioxide and ozone. Less plentiful are the ones we help con-
tribute to the equation: methane, nitrous oxide and chlorofluorocarbons.

Is the nature guy right? Is this enhanced greenhouse effect
overheating the planet, as in global warming? Sure, but it's
part of the equation we've already covered; our planet is in
a warming phase—and warmer begets more reactive gasses
as bacteria in wetlands and oceans increase and produce
more methane and nitrous oxide. Better warm than cold;
a return of the Little Ice Age would be a bad thing. A good
thing would be to cut down on those gasses we help introduce into the atmosphere—methane, nitrous oxide and
chlorofluorocarbons.

Methane is produced by bacterial action in wetlands, by cattle,
pig manure, rice paddies, coal and gas emissions, and aquatic
upheaval of trapped gas.

Nitrous oxide is formed by bacterial action in soil and oceans,
production and application of nitrogen fertilizers, livestock,
the manufacture of nylon and the burning of fossil fuels.
This gas is the main, naturally occurring regulator of stratospheric ozone and the fourth largest contributor to greenhouse gasses.

Chlorofluorocarbons, or more commonly called by their brand name Freon, are organic compounds that include chlorine, a major contributor to ozone depletion. A refrigerant, the gas is banned in civilized countries, but is still widely used in many not-so-civilized countries.

I have a scientist friend who swears that the millions of dinosaurs helped in their own extinction by continuously farting methane gas. Don't laugh, he is very convincing. He thinks their flatulence raised the methane content of the atmosphere and made it vulnerable to flash fires from a huge asteroid impact. The giant asteroid exploded debris into the very limits of the atmosphere and into a spreading orbit. When gravity returned this mist of debris, atmospheric friction caused it to catch fire and ignite methane in the troposphere, causing immense flash fires that destroyed forests. Another extinction theory, and one of many, but geologists have discovered extensive belts of carbon in sedimentary rock from the extinction period. Something burned the forests big time, and smoke from such widespread fires might have temporarily cancelled out the greenhouse effect and returned the earth to its normal temperature of $-18°C$. The big lizards would have frozen, while the small furry mammals could have survived by huddling together in burrows. Makes sense, but we will have to wait for geologists to map that layer of carbon to get the whole picture. Regardless, it's clear that some similar cataclysmic event occurred that made furry little mammals our ancestors and not those ugly reptiles.

Is enhanced greenhouse effect melting the Arctic and Antarctic icecaps? Sure, but what the media doomsayers don't tell you is that it's a reoccurring effect. While we sat on our hands, the Russians kept records on Arctic conditions starting in 1880, and from them we get perspective.

ARCTIC OASIS

From 1880 to 1940, Arctic temperatures rose and ice melted, and from 1940 to 1960, Arctic temperatures fell and ice froze, and from 1960 to the present, temps are on the rise again. It's a natural cycle, and if indeed the seas rise for a while, which they have before, the world will simply have to adapt. There are too many people on this planet, and far too many inhabit low places. Rising sea levels will see a gradual move of populations to higher ground, and if governments have any sense, they will already be planning the "where to."

Rising water levels and a warming climate should afford Canadians some wonderful opportunities. Port cities like Halifax and Vancouver with already nearly perfect harbours will become larger, and shallow-water ports will have deeper water. Agricultural hardiness zones will slowly advance northward, allowing unsuitable areas to be turned into viable farmland, and Churchill, Manitoba, will have open water year-round for shipping increased grain production. Arctic port cities will spring up to service both the oil industry and the passing parade of ships using the Northwest Passage.

Some doors will close, but many will open.

Cloud Primer

Clouds are either cumulus or stratus; the former is puffed up by rising warm air, the latter is a high-altitude fog created by air that doesn't rise. Clouds are further divided into four altitudes: towering, high, middle and low.

Towering clouds can rise to over 25,000 metres and behave badly; these black hats often have the Latin word *nimbus* (rain cloud) tacked on so you know not to walk the dog. If you see one of these in the neighbourhood, stay inside.

High clouds, or alto, are composed of tiny ice crystals and are found at altitudes of 6000 to 9000 metres. These are divided into three types: cirrus, sometimes called "mare's tails," look like wispy streaks of white in a blue sky; cirrocumulus, sometimes called a "mackerel sky," look rippled and wavy; and cirrostratus, which are thin, high-altitude gossamer sheets composed of ice crystals and are responsible for halos around the sun or moon.

Middle clouds are divided into alto or cumulus and are found at altitudes between 2000 and 6000 metres. Altostratus are dense sheets of grey but can appear as stripes. The sun or moon is visible but looks hazy. Altocumulus are composed of water droplets and resemble mare's tails but are larger and puffier. The sun shines through, but often has a corona that can be in various colours.

Low clouds begin at around 1800 metres and have three types: stratus, nimbo and strato.

Stratus is a thick grey fog covering the entire sky and responsible for drizzling rain. These clouds form when there is little or no vertical movement of air.

Nimbostratus are rain clouds. These are dark, ominous and sometimes touch the ground. Nimbostrati are actually middle clouds with low bases and occurring precipitation but can belong to any grouping because their vertical extension can be massive.

Stratocumulus are irregular masses of various shades of grey spread out in layers. No rain from these clouds, but they bear watching since they sometimes fuse into nimbostratus and cause sudden downpours.

Cumulonimbus are the ones to watch. Bases may touch the ground and updrafts rise to over 25,000 metres. High winds aloft can sometimes cleave their tops so they resemble a black-smith's anvil. Thunderstorms and tornadoes spawn from these clouds. They also produce positive lightning strikes, so don't walk the dog.

Cumulus are fine-weather clouds, unless they come together and form a cumulonimbus, but that doesn't happen often since the average lifespan of a cumulus cloud is only 15 minutes.

Here is a list of cloud types preceded by their metrological designation letters—handy for reading online weather maps.

Cloud Types
AC—altocumulus
ACC—altocumulus castellanus
AS—altostratus
CC—cirrocumulus
CS—cirrostratus

CI—cirrus
CB—cumulonimbus
CU—cumulus
CF—cumulus fractus
SF—stratus fractus
TCU—towering cumulus
NS—nimbostratus
SC—stratocumulus
ST—stratus
F—fog
R—rain
A—hail
IP—ice pellets (including ice pellet showers)
L—drizzle (including freezing drizzle)
IC—ice crystals
S—snow (snow showers, snow pellets and snow grains)
BS—blowing snow
D—dust, blowing dust or dust storm
H—haze
N—sand, blowing sand or sand storm
K—smoke
VA—volcanic ash

Atmospheric Primer

Our atmosphere consists of five layers, three of which have boundaries: the troposphere, and tropopause boundary; stratosphere, and stratosphere boundary; mesosphere, and mesosphere boundary; thermosphere; and exosphere.

- Troposphere is the stuff we breathe and where all the weather comes from. It rises to about eight kilometres at the poles and 18 kilometres at the equator. This zone contains most of the atmospheric mass and almost all the water vapour. In the upper reaches of this sphere are found

the Rossby waves, strong undulating winds moving east to west on a global scale—better known as the westerlies. Tropopause boundary is a temperature inversion lying atop the troposphere in a narrow broken band that loosely extends from pole to pole. This is the point where air ceases to cool with altitude and begins to warm. In this boundary between troposphere and stratosphere are born the jet streams.

- Stratosphere extends upwards from the troposphere for roughly 50 kilometres and is almost entirely void of weather. Jet pilots like it for that reason and because the air is thin and offers little resistance to the aircraft. When you see a jet contrail, know it's there because the planes engines are adding weather to the void—moisture from the exhaust freezes and forms ice crystals that will eventually float down into the troposphere. Stratopause is the boundary between the stratosphere and mesosphere, at a height of 50 to 55 kilometres, and is the point where temperatures rising with altitude reach maximums.

- Mesosphere extends upward from the stratosphere for roughly 80 kilometres and contains minute amounts of water vapour and gasses—it can be –100°C at the top and is the sphere where meteors burn up. At night, when you observe a shooting star, you are looking at the mesosphere. Satellite pictures of our planet all portray a narrow, dark blue band around the outer edge, and that is the mesosphere.

- Thermosphere, sometimes called the ionosphere, is nearly empty space. Gas particles found here become ionized from constant exposure to cosmic rays, meaning their atoms are stripped of protons and electrons. They have no pizzazz and drift in lifeless layers that extend upwards for 330 kilometres. It's because of these layers that we can send radio messages from beyond the horizon—they bounce off and reflect down. Higher frequency waves, such as those used in FM radio and television transmissions, are not affected and will travel through the layers and into space. Temperature extremes abound in this zone; daytime temperatures can exceed 1400°C.

- Exosphere is up, up, and away empty. Lonesome gas particles drifting here are as hot as the sun during day and almost absolute zero at night, around –274°C. Any gas molecules found here are so far apart they rarely collide and attain tremendous speeds. Oxygen and helium molecules rising into the exosphere pick up so much speed they escape earth's gravity and head into space.

Wind Primer

Build it, and they will come. A motion picture cliché that pretty much describes how most local winds are caused. Altocumulus clouds build inside a low-pressure cell, and surrounding air rushes in like to a vacuum cleaner. It builds, and the air comes, and if the clouds are big, high and fast moving, it will come at gale-force speed.

> Hey, Martha! This writer guy has lost me. What's a gale?

A gale is a strong wind with speeds of 62 to 74 kilometres per hour. Gale is number 8 on the Beaufort Wind Scale (a 0 to 12 scale devised in 1805 by Rear-Admiral Sir Francis Beaufort to enable sea captains to describe wind affect). A modernized version is still in use today for describing what winds do at different speeds; our number 8, now called a fresh gale, causes moderate waves and spindrift (foam) to fly from the tops—on land it causes twigs to snap and cars to veer. Zero on the Beaufort scale is a flat sea with no wind, while 12 is a hurricane: huge waves, air filled with spindrift, sea completely white with driving spray and visibility greatly reduced. Old Admiral Beaufort must have scratched that number 12 into the logbook next to his last will and testament.

Local winds flow from areas of high pressure to low, while global winds are caused by solar heat absorption differentials between climate zones and the rotation of the earth. This rotation causes centrifugal force, which bends winds towards the west in the Northern Hemisphere and to the east in the Southern Hemisphere. Called "Coriolis effect," this centrifugal bending, as seen when water swirls down a drain, is responsible for the rotation of cyclones and tornadoes. Draining water swirls counter-clockwise in the Northern Hemisphere, clockwise in the south, and goes straight down at the equator.

This differential heating also causes local winds, such as sea breezes, where water continues to give off heat as the land cools causing a rapid circulation of air. Mountain breezes are caused by similar heating differential; mountain slopes get first light and more heat than valleys and pull up cooler air, but in the afternoon the roles are reversed and air is drawn down by the sun-warmed valleys.

There are three primary atmospheric circulation cells, the Hadley, Ferrel and Polar cells.

Hadley circulation is confined to the equatorial region and produces tropical easterly winds both above and below the equator that converge to form the trade winds. Ferrel circulation is confined to the upper latitudes and produces prevailing westerly winds, while Polar circulation provides polar easterlies. Narrow global wind belts called jet streams are found between these Big Kahuna circulation cells, and at very high altitudes.

Wind is our friend; it heats and cools us, provides locomotion and power, but often it acts badly and tears up a few trailer parks, and sometimes it can get downright beastly and tear up whole countries. Atlantic hurricanes shred Caribbean island countries on a regular basis, but their residents have learned to adapt. Years ago, when I first visited one of these islands,

I couldn't help notice the rows of tiny, different-coloured houses with corrugated metal roofs. I thought them madly quaint, but a subsequent visit, hard on the heels of a hurricane, revealed the reasons behind the quaintness. Most of the island looked a shambles, but somehow those rows of colourful little houses had escaped being damaged. Curious about their sturdiness, I asked a friend, who explained that the quaint dwellings had indeed been smashed along with everything else but were rebuilt in a day. The owners simply walked about after the blow and retrieved their particular colour of building material. As for the corrugated metal roofs, they were all the same size, so any one they found did nicely. Island people endure hurricanes almost every season and, for most, have become just another of life's inconveniences—the mighty oak falls, but the willow endures.

Some winds have personality and names; British Columbia has the Qualicum and infamous Squamish winds, while the Prairies have the Alberta Clipper and beloved Chinook winds, with both of these having connections to a wind called the Pineapple Express. Also known as the Pineapple Connection, this wind is characterized by a strong, steady flow of moist air from the waters adjacent to the Hawaiian Islands. It's a precipitation pipeline, extending all the way from Hawaii to the northwest coast of North America. The Pineapple Express is driven by a strong, southern branch of the polar jet stream and is marked by the presence of a slow or stationary frontal boundary. Pineapple Express systems can bring deluge, especially to the province of British Columbia.

Pineapple Express systems can also generate heavy snowfall in the mountains of British Columbia, but it's usually transient and melted quickly by the warming effect of the system. After being drained of moisture, a Pineapple Express system may

reach the Canadian prairies as a Chinook and treat residents to a taste of the tropics and a brief respite from winter.

Not to be outdone, East Coasters have literally dozens of pet names for winds: Wreckhouse, Sheila's brush, siwash, screecher, shuff, airsome and, my favourite, the fairy wind.

The rustle of the wind reminds us a Fairy is near.

–Unknown

Wreckhouse winds rate a special mention for their ferocity (in case you're planning an RV trip around the East Coast). Arriving in Newfoundland by ferry, at Channel Port-aux-Basque, will have you traversing the Wreckhouse (there's no way around it), a flat moor area between the Long Range

Mountains and the sea. It's those mountains that create problems; when a southeast storm wind funnels through its rocky crags, gulches and canyons, it becomes compressed. Once free of the mountains and onto the Wreckhouse, the air is uncompressed and picks up amazing speed; gusts in excess of 200 kilometres per hour are common. Nowhere on the North American continent will you find winds like at the Wreckhouse—they can have the intensity of a Category 2 hurricane and blow your car or RV clean off the road. These winds occur mostly in the spring and fall seasons, and drivers are usually forewarned by the first overturned tractor-trailer.

Don't laugh, it happens all the time. In the old days, when Newfoundland had a railway, the wind flipped railcars off the track on a regular basis. It got so bad that the rail company hired Lockland "Lockie" MacDougal to monitor the winds and warn trains. The rail company created a folk hero, and many a rail traveller owed his life to Lockie "the human wind gauge" MacDougal. Lockie is gone now, as is the train, and today's travellers must rely on a local anemometer for wind warning, a meteorological device that employs spinning, wind-catching cups to record speeds.

Note: Be warned, a reservation is required for the six-hour ferry crossing from Sydney, Nova Scotia, to Channel Port-aux-Basque. On rare occasions, Wreckhouse winds can force the incoming ferry to weather out the storm in the shelter of the Anguilla Mountains, some 50 kilometres away.

As foul as those southeastern winds can be at the Wreckhouse, the most feared winds in Newfoundland and along the entire East Coast are the dreaded nor'easters. These winds are caused when large, low-pressure cells moving northeast across the U.S. encounter the warm, moist air of the Atlantic. These cells often explode into huge rain and snowstorms that have earned them the name "bomb cyclones." They can grow to tremendous size as they move offshore and drive northeast. Winds in these bomb cyclones rotate counter-clockwise, so foul weather is usually accompanied by a strong northeast-blowing wind…a nor'easter. Most nor'easters are born from high-pressure cells originating in the U.S., but some are caused by winds called Alberta Clippers, high-pressure cells that form in the lee of the Rocky Mountains. These fast-moving cells of dry, cold air move southeast and sometimes reach the Atlantic where they become bomb cyclones and turn northeast.

However, it was a more southerly storm from Indiana that supplied the catalyst for the most famous nor'easter, the October 28, 1991 "perfect storm" featured in the Hollywood movie of the same name. That storm cell nosed into the Atlantic some 600 kilometres south of Halifax, Nova Scotia, and struck out across that province as an extratropical cyclone, a hurricane not formed in the tropics. Meanwhile, out in the Atlantic, a tropical hurricane called Grace had moved up the coast causing damage galore. Responding to the huge low created by the extratropical, Grace pulled a hard left turn and managed to spin off a storm cell that collided with both the extratropical and cold air moving down from the Canadian Arctic. Grace was spent, but with lots of warm, moist air, she energized the two colliding cells, got absorbed and became part of a new hurricane that moved south over the Gulf current where it gathered energy and created the highest waves ever recorded on the Nova Scotia shelf.

This newly energized monster then moved northeast and made landfall in Nova Scotia as a dangerous extratropical storm. This was the legendary perfect storm of movie fame, a hurricane with no name that east coasters call "the Halloween Storm." That storm was costly, and altogether (in the U.S. and Canada) accounted for damages of almost $1 billion and caused 12 fatalities, including the six crewmen of the fishing vessel the *Andrea Gail* featured in the movie.

Just over a year later, during the first few days of December 1992, and like it was playing a game of one-upmanship, another nor'easter battered the northeastern coast of the U.S., killing 19 people and causing $2 billion in damages. Slow as molasses, that storm edged northeast, skimming Canada's Maritime provinces and dumping over 26 centimetres of snow on Sydney, Nova Scotia. That storm was foul, but not as catastrophic as the following year's game, when one of our Alberta Clippers got helped into the U.S. Midwest by a low-flying polar jet stream and smacked into a huge low coming up from the Gulf of Mexico. Driven southeast by the jet stream, that unruly mass of air rolled onto the southern Atlantic on March 12, 1993, and exploded into a humongous storm that stretched from our Maritime provinces to Central America. It flattened Cuba and the Florida Panhandle, and showed folks in 26 American states and most of eastern Canada that cold arctic air and unlimited water vapour is a deadly combination. Temperatures plummeted, and a screaming nor'easter pelted the eastern seaboard with blinding snow all the way from Florida to Newfoundland. It killed 300 people and cut the power to 10 million homes. It closed airports from the Maritimes to Florida, brought road traffic to a standstill and buried small towns and villages. Five days later, on March 17, the legendary Great Blizzard of '93, thought by some to be another perfect storm, moved out to sea, leaving in its wake an estimated 25 billion tons of snow.

Jet Streams

These east-to-west, high-speed ribbons of air originate in the troposphere boundary and are formed by the deflection of upper winds by Coriolis acceleration. Jet streams travel in high altitudes, weaving and dipping like snakes. Canada's main concern is with the most northerly of these winds—the polar jet stream, a fast-moving whip of frigid air that can create troughs of low pressure and ridges of high pressure even at high altitudes. Bad enough, but dipping closer to the ground it becomes a low-level jet stream and may cause severe weather mischief when encountering warm air masses coming from the southwest. Thunderstorms, tornadoes and ice storms can result from a low flyer—even worse is a split, with one side heading south and pressing up wet air from the Caribbean. That has happened a number of times, and on each occasion there's been hell to pay—the last and biggest payment being the Great Ice Storm of 1998.

During summer, the average location of the polar jet stream over central Canada is about 50° N latitude. In winter, it arcs northward over BC, forms a ridge over the province and then turns sharply southward over the Great Plains of the U.S. It then plunges as far south as northern Texas before curving northeastward over the Mississippi River valley. Finally, it wends its way eastward and leaves North America, heading over New England or Atlantic Canada.

Below the polar stream, and approximately 13 kilometres above the subtropical high-pressure zone, can be found another easterly blowing wind snake, the subtropical jet stream. The reason for its formation is similar to the polar jet stream, but the subtropical stream is weaker because of the lower latitudinal temperature and pressure gradient.

Jet streams can also be isolated phenomena called jet streaks. Rising and sinking air found upstream and downstream from jet streaks may cause dangerous thunderstorm activity, and these are monitored closely by weather services.

Note: Jet stream monitoring maps can be found online.

The National Climate

*There is bad weather, and there is dangerous
weather, and in the North, it's critical you know
the difference between the two.*

–Willy Laserich, famous Canadian medevac pilot

ARCTIC OUTBREAKS

The Great White North

Most Canadians live within a few hundred kilometres of our cross-country rail system and think the North is the edge of nothing and a place where lumber and mining companies get stuff. In essence, most Canadians think they reside in a country that is over 5000 kilometres long and only 200 or 300 kilometres wide. That is the long and skinny of the national thought process, and who cares what happens up north as long as nobody steals it when we're not looking? Americans like to visit us, mostly to get stuff, and they are positive the far north is an edge, the edge of a new economic bonanza. They would like to steal our Arctic, as would the Russians, Norwegians and Swedes. What's up there worth stealing?

Canada's future is up there, a quicker way to the Pacific, and perhaps half the world's oil reserves.

Our Arctic is an ice-covered landmass of islands surrounded by water—navigable water, if not frozen solid year-round. But hey, the tail end of the Quaternary (the last Ice Age) has delivered us an economic miracle—the ice is melting. A bad thing, say the Americans, Russians, Swedes and Norwegians, who send ships and submarines to study the phenomena and map the seabed around our islands. They're up there like bad teeth, and we haven't the muscle to yank them out. In the end, we may have to share our future. An unfortunate situation, because all we had to do was keep our eyes open and the flag flying. But it's a cold, barren, inhospitable place, and until a few decades ago, only indigenous peoples had any interest in flying flags.

How cold is it? Well, that is hard to say since we only started keeping accurate records in 1960, but the available averages are –32°C for the winter months with occasionally dips to –50°C. A nice place to visit, but only the arctic air mass wants to live there, and even it likes an occasional trip south, sometimes getting a cold finger all the way to Mexico.

It's another brother and sister act, the continental and maritime arctic air masses. In winter, the sea is locked in ice, and 24-hour nights combine to cool the dry air to subzero temps, known as the "continental arctic air mass." During summer months, the reverse happens: the open sea and long days warm and humidify the air. It's still cold, but with plenty of sunshine to walk the dog, and that is the "maritime arctic air mass."

During winter months, the frigid continental arctic air mass becomes increasingly larger and often spills out into the lower latitudes in what meteorologists call an outbreak.

These downward rampages can occur at any month, but happen most often in winter, early spring or late fall, and get generally noted in newspapers as "killer frosts." Arctic outbreaks are often economic mini disasters as they cause late and early crops to fail and our population to use more heating oil. Good for oil companies, but bad for Canadians forced to cough up for the shortfalls in oil, winter wheat, veggies and fruit.

Arctic outbreaks can be far reaching. In February 1889, a Canadian outbreak reached all the way to the Texas Panhandle, causing temperatures to fall to –30°C, an all-time record. Residents of Galveston, Texas, accustomed to a temperate climate, awoke in the morning to find a thin sheet of ice on their harbour, an amazing sight never seen again.

That year of 1889 was a foul-weather time for Americans; a few months after the Texas freeze, on May 31, a meandering Midwest thunderstorm ran up against the Allegany Mountains and began dumping torrential rain on the area around the town of Johnstown, Pennsylvania. A standing joke in Johnstown was the poor condition of a dam belonging to the South Fork Fishing and Hunting Club. But on June 1, that joke died along with over 2200 residents when incessant rainfall caused the dam to break and a wall of debris to roar down on Johnstown like a giant steam roller. Since that was America's all-time worst flood disaster, most Canadians are aware of the Johnstown flood, but what they probably don't know is that the town got flooded numerous times after the big one, resulting in hundreds more fatalities. Some people never learn.

The Johnstown flood has little to do with outbreaks, except that the town sits in a river flood plain, and cities and towns built in those places are vulnerable to sudden weather changes

Hey, Martha! Is this guy off his track? What's the Johnstown flood got to do with Arctic outbreaks?

that breakouts cause. The Johnstown flood was a disaster waiting to happen and might well have been caused by the next breakout of cold arctic air aggravating a migrating Caribbean warm cell. Arctic outbreaks cause dramatic changes in local weather systems that must be anticipated: not building on flood plains is a major anticipation, while keeping dikes and dams in good order is another. Two lessons learned the hard way by more than one Canadian city. Winnipeg endured so many floods that it finally smartened up and now has a system of dikes to divert an overabundance of Red River around the city. The river still floods, but damage to the city is minimized. Toronto suffered terrible floods caused by Hurricane Hazel and immediately after set up a flood control agency that bought flood-plain properties and banned future construction in flood-sensitive areas. Wise moves that have paid big dividends, because when weather is concerned, what goes around always comes around.

Weird Phenomena

Shoot for the moon. Even if you miss, you'll land among the stars.

—Les Brown, motivational speaker

HOT AND COLD

The Coldest Day

In Snag, Yukon Territory, on February 3, 1947, its 40 or so residents, mostly airport personnel, awoke to a normal sub-arctic morning: a sky filled with stars (short days in winter) and cold air. But by mid-morning that air got appreciably colder, and the employees working the airport began tapping the thermometer. Something wasn't right, and by the next morning that something turned unreadable since the markings on the alcohol column thermometer did not go low enough. It was only after the thermometer was marked and sent off for measurement did the residents find that their tiny outpost had set a North American record for low temperature, −62.8°C.

You can't help but visualize the control tower operators dumping pots of water over the side to experience the explosive effect before it hit ground. Laughing, hollering, having a great old time, until they discovered frozen plumbing and bare skin freezes in two or three minutes. You can also imagine them contacting headquarters in Toronto for advice and receiving back the standard Russian model. Don't wear your glasses—they'll freeze to your face.

The Hottest Days

The deadliest heat wave in Canadian history owed its existence to a strong high-pressure ridge that set up on America's West Coast at the end of June 1936. That ridge had muscle and pushed dry, hot air northeast across America's drought-stricken Midwest, the so-called dustbowl states. Poor farming practices had turned once fertile prairie lands into lifeless hardscrabble susceptible to wind erosion and solar heating. Desert topography, and that hardscrabble added more heat to already hot air, like feeding a blast furnace. Nothing to worry about—people down the line were used to heat waves. A few nights sleeping on the porch was only a minor inconvenience and considered a rite of summer. But that summer of '36 would be different, and in the midst of the Great Depression, people across the U.S. and Canada suffered record heat for a record number of days, and 5000 lost their lives.

The heat would not go away, and those few nights sleeping on the porch turned unbearable. By July people took to the basements or didn't sleep at all, and as the heat wave stretched into the Great Lakes states, it withered crops and baked ripening fruit on trees. In Ohio, temperatures soared to 43°C, and the wave just kept sizzling onward towards the East Coast, where the states of New York and New Jersey suffered record temps and many fatalities.

Along the way to the U.S. East Coast, the great heat wave soaked up water from the Great Lakes and reached up into Manitoba and Ontario. For two weeks, temperatures stayed at 44°C, though humidity made it feel much hotter. The persistent high temperatures left almost 800 Canadians dead from heat exhaustion, and another 400 died from heat-related factors that included folks drowning while seeking refuge in rivers or lakes. According to Environment Canada, the heat was so intense that steel rails and bridge girders twisted, sidewalks buckled and paved roads melted into goop.

Hot stuff, but it's about more than just temperature; it's about how hot it feels, or the humidex. The humidex is an index, or calculated value, which describes how hot saturated air actually feels. The humidex is a Canadian innovation, first used in 1965 to combine air temperature and humidity into one number to reflect how the temperature is perceived. The 44°C temperatures in that 1936 heat wave probably felt more like an unbearable 54°C. When ambient air becomes saturated with water vapour, sweat evaporates slowly, and those people around in 1936 must have felt hot, sticky and about to die.

Residents of Canada's southern areas can get very uncomfortable even without continental heat waves, especially those folks in Windsor, Ontario, when on June 20, 1953, the humidex reached 52.1°C. Unbelievably hot, considering Environment Canada marks any reading over 40°C as extreme heat.

Here is a guide to humidex comfort levels, according to the Meteorological Service of Canada:

- Less than 29°C: no discomfort
- 30 to 39°C: some discomfort
- 40 to 45°C: great discomfort; avoid exertion
- Above 45°C: dangerous
- Above 54°C: heat stroke imminent

Extreme heat warnings are issued when the combination of heat, humidity and other weather conditions can be very dangerous.

Heat-related Illnesses

Heat exhaustion occurs when people exercise heavily or work in a hot and humid place, and body fluids are lost through heavy sweating. Blood flow to the skin increases, and blood flow to vital organs decreases, resulting in a form of mild shock. If the condition goes untreated, the body temperature will continue to rise and the person may suffer heatstroke.

When a person's temperature control system (sweating to cool down the body) doesn't work, and heat exhaustion progresses to heatstroke, body temperature can rise so high that it can cause brain damage and death if not cooled quickly.

What exactly is too hot? Environment Canada issues extreme hot weather warnings when the air temperature is more than 30°C and the humidex is more than 40°C.

Municipalities also issue heat alerts, but the criteria varies. For example, in Toronto, heat and extreme heat alerts are issued by the city's chief medical officer of health. These are ratings of how the weather affects human health, based on historical mortality data and meteorological data. Heat alerts are issued when a hot air mass is forecast and the likelihood of deaths is more than 65 percent. An extreme heat alert is broadcast when the heat has become more severe or is expected to last longer, and the likelihood of deaths is more than 90 percent.

In 2001, Toronto became the first Canadian city to issue heat warnings; as of July 5, 2006, that city has issued 38 heat warnings and 29 extreme heat warnings.

So how can a person cope with the heat?

To avoid heat-related illnesses, air-conditioned spaces—such as shopping malls and libraries—are good places to seek relief. If that is not possible, or you must venture outside during extremely hot temperatures, here are some tips:

- Stay hydrated. Drink lots of water and natural fruit juices, even if you don't feel thirsty. Avoid alcoholic beverages, coffee and cola.

- Avoid going out in the blazing sun or heat when possible. Seek shade as much as possible, or plan excursions for the early morning or evening.

- Cover up. Wear a hat and loose-fitting, light clothing.

- Reduce the heat. Keep the drapes drawn and blinds closed. Keep the lights off or turned down low.

- Cool down with baths or showers periodically, or use cool, wet towels.

- Avoid intense or moderately intense physical activity.

- Be aware that fans alone may not be enough when the temperatures are high.

SOME WEIRD, BUT NICE, THINGS

Snow Rollers

You wake up, glance out the window at the fresh snowfall and stop dead in your tracks. Your front lawn is dotted with snowballs, big ones. These things are fun and require just the right snow conditions to form; as any kid knows, the making of snowballs and snowmen requires packing snow. But no kid has rolled the weird balls on your front lawn; the wind is responsible. Bits of snow breaking off in a stiff breeze get bounced along, gather other bits and grow larger—a rolling stone gathering moss, except it is snow. Snow rollers are usually cylindrical in shape, hollow, and sit there looking like invitations to come make snowmen. Dogs are crazy about them; they run around jumping on as many as they can and have a great old time—if only dogs could laugh.

Moon Bows

Rainbows occur when rain droplets refract sunshine. If the moon is full and low in the sky, it may treat you to the same phenomena, but it's called a moon bow. They are not as bright as rainbows but are so ethereal you can actually believe there's a pot of gold at the end. Moon bows are not that rare, and when conditions are right, you'll see one and think you've found a pot of gold.

Sun Dogs or Parhelia

Three suns? You might see them and question your sanity. But you're all right, Jack, they are just halos. Like rainbows, sun dogs are caused by reflected sunshine, but instead of water droplets, the reflective surfaces are high-altitude ice crystals aligned horizontally to the sun. Most sun dogs are white, but sometimes they exhibit a spectrum of colours: red closest to the sun, to a pale bluish tail stretching away from the sun. White sun dogs occur when sunlight reflects off atmospheric ice crystals, and coloured sun dogs by light refracted *through* them. White sun dogs can also be caused by sunlight reflecting off water on the ground and focusing onto the clouds above.

A few sun dog events have become famous. In Nuremberg, Germany, on April 14, 1561, the skies filled with a multitude of celestial objects observed by thousands of people. These objects were portrayed in a 1566 woodcut by the artist Hans Glaser, called the 1561 Nuremberg Event. The phenomenon he depicted resemble the types of events that occur as Parhelia (sun dogs), halos and floating ice crystals called diamond dust.

Diamond Dust

Ice crystals are most obvious when forming halos around the sun or moon. But they can also appear as precipitation and make you a believer in enchanted lands and fairies. These ice crystals form in high cirrus clouds and tumble to earth through clear skies reflecting sunshine like tiny diamonds. It is an enchanting phenomena to witness, especially when the air is still and the crystals hang in the air nearly motionless. When this occurs, it turns adults into small children and children into the happiest beings on the planet. You will see diamond dust mostly in the Arctic, and to experience both diamond dust and the northern lights will have you flying the flag and not wanting to leave.

Aurora Borealis

Northern lights to Canadians, aurora australis to those Down Under, and a great show in either hemisphere—the dance of the wispy veils that people will sit and watch for hours. Green is the most common colour, but red, blue and violet have been observed. These shimmering lights are caused by particles from the sun colliding with gas molecules in our thermosphere, sometimes called the ionosphere. When solar particles collide with those atmospheric gases, the collision energy between the solar particle and the gas molecule emits as a photon—a light particle. When there are millions of collisions, you have an aurora—lights that may seem to move across the sky. Northern lights occur in southern areas of Canada about three times per year and in the far north about six times per month. The best viewing seasons are late fall and early spring, but if the reader is really intent on seeing the show, hop on a plane to Andenes, Norway, where they dance almost every night.

Note: You can find great websites featuring aurora borealis photographs on the Internet.

Noctilucent Clouds

The sun has set, no moon, but there is an amazing light in the sky. Sometimes coloured, sometimes moving, these can look intriguingly like a UFO. If you see one, relax; it's the sun reflecting off an extremely high cloud, around 80 to 100 kilometres high and probably composed of ice crystals sticking to both meteor and volcanic dusts. Civil authorities hate these clouds, because reports of UFO sightings pour into their offices after every appearance. That aside, anyone who spots one of these clouds is thoroughly impressed, as they are a magnificent phenomenon. First sighted by sunset watchers in 1885, two years after the massive eruption of a volcano called Krakatoa, the clouds persisted after the volcano-inspired sunsets had stopped, and over the years have spread.

Astronauts can see noctilucent clouds from outer space and often wax poetic about the wondrous, electric blue clouds that waft in the very fringes of outer space. Why these clouds are in the mesosphere is a mystery, as no water vapour exists in that sphere to produce ice crystals. Theories as to their origin abound, but most centre on volcanic and meteor dust gathering up traces of induced water vapour like tiny dust mops—water probably introduced into the sphere via volcanic eruptions and rocket contrails.

Nacreous Clouds

These are other super-high stratospheric clouds, around 20 to 40 kilometres high, that may contain water mixed with nitric and sulphuric acids and cause destruction of ozone molecules. These clouds are rare and appear in skies as a band of vivid pastel colours. Both noctilucent and nacreous clouds are fast movers and have been recorded travelling in excess of 750 kilometres per hour.

Sometimes called mother-of-pearl, nacreous clouds are mostly visible within two hours after sunset or before dawn when they blaze with bright and slowly shifting iridescent colours. They are gossamer sheets of clouds that slowly furl and unfurl in the darkening sky putting on a spectacular show.

Lenticular Clouds

These clouds form when air of varying moisture content is pushed over a mountain or large hill and encounters stalled air called standing waves. Pushed-up air will then continue the rise and form into layers according to their moisture content: dry air at the top, wet at the bottom. Lenticular clouds are usually lens shaped and are sometimes mistaken for a UFO, but they can also resemble a large stack of dishes or hamburgers. These clouds indicate strong air turbulence and are avoided by aircraft, except for glider pilots who actively seek them out for rising air. If a vacation to Hawaii is in your future, Mauna Kea, Hawaii's tallest mountain, is a good place to observe these weird cloud formations.

Sun Pillars

These can be startling phenomena and have you thinking UFO. The sun is rising or setting and suddenly there is a giant beam of bright light rising from the earth. Relax. What you're seeing is sunlight reflecting off millions of ice crystals rotating on their vertical axis. Sun pillars are neat, and can sometimes rise to 20 degrees above the horizon, and while mostly white, they can sometimes treat audiences to a display of vivid colours. These optical illusions can be red, yellow or purple, and oftentimes hang around for an hour or so after sunset. The formation of a sun pillar can be compared with the glitter path caused by the setting sun reflecting on a wavy water surface. Look for them; they're not rare and occur about 30 times per year in most places.

Fire Rainbow, or Circumhorizontal Arc

These resemble a rainbow set aflame and appear when atmospheric-suspended ice crystals in a high-altitude cirrus cloud are in proper alignment with the sun. Ice crystals are hexagonal, prism shaped, and sunlight must enter through a side facet and exit from a bottom. If conditions are optimal, light refraction will transform the entire cloud into a flaming rainbow. A not-to-be-missed optical display, but alas, so rare you'll probably never see one except in a photograph. National Geographic has a good one on their website.

Crepuscular Rays

Sunbursts—sometimes called the Fingers of God or Jacob's Ladder—are optical effects caused by sunlight streaming through holes in clouds and made visible by particulates or water vapour in the atmosphere. Crepuscular rays appear to converge on the sun, and if they converge in the opposite direction, they're called anti-crepuscular rays. Like crepuscular rays, these are parallel shafts of sunlight from holes in the clouds, and their opposing direction is simple perspective. A wide road converges towards the horizon, but turn around and it converges to the opposite horizon.

Airglow

Airglow is why night is never absolute darkness. Our atmosphere creates light, not much, but enough to see your hand in front of your face at night. It does this in various ways: the recombining of ions split apart by sunlight; cosmic rays entering the exosphere; or by simple chemical luminescence, as when atoms of oxygen and nitrogen combine to form a molecule of nitrous oxide and emit a photon. Airglow enabled our early settlers to find their outhouses in the dark and was considered another of God's gifts to man. But modern astronomers, forced to send their telescopes into space to avoid airglow, have a different slant and consider it an expensive curse from somewhere else.

Green Flash

Vacationers look for it religiously—the legendary emerald-coloured flash of light that occurs seconds before sunrise or sunset. Some people swear it doesn't exist, but don't believe them; it's there all right, but only for a second, so don't blink. Green flash occurs because sunshine is curved slightly and refracted by our atmosphere; high-frequency light (green and blue) curves most and is what we see first at sunrise, or last if you are watching at night. However, the horizon must be clear of clouds to see the flash, and in the humid tropics, where most people watch for it, the green flash is a rare atmospheric condition. Of course, this explains why some folks swear it doesn't exist. If you are adamant about seeing the green flash, make the Sahara or Mojave deserts your next vacation destination.

Moving and Don't Know Where To?

Until I came to Canada, I never knew "snow" was a four-letter word.

–Alberto Manguel

THIS LIST MAY HELP YOU DECIDE

How about moving to Estevan, Saskatchewan, or Medicine Hat, Alberta? These are Canada's twin sunshine cities, and both average around 2500 hours of sunshine per year. Estevan also has the highest annual number of hours per year of clear skies (between zero and two-tenths sky cover): 2979 hours.

The Sunniest Big City

There are no rusty spurs in Calgary, Alberta, not with an average 333 perfect days. Surprised? Most people are, but it's true, and for two reasons: one, because it's downwind from

Hey, Martha! Let's move to some place with lots of sunshine.

the Rocky Mountains—airflow over Calgary has been freed of water vapour and is usually dry as toast. Secondly, the city receives more sunshine—solar radiation has been mapped for all of North America and shows a strong belt of radiation crossing the U.S. plains states with a hump extending northward into Canada's heartland. Good for crops, good for the Calgary Stampede, and good for you because it doesn't snow or rain much in Calgary. But it can get extremely cold, so better take along your mittens.

Even winters in Calgary have a bright side, and that's called a Chinook, a warm wind blowing down from the mountains. This wind is really a Foehn wind, but called a Chinook in memory of the almost extinct First Nation band that once inhabited the area. Chinooks can raise winter temps as much as 20°C and are much loved by residents who lend the name to almost everything: dogs, cars, beer, motels, good eats and hockey teams.

Like It Hot?

Kamloops, British Columbia, has the hottest summers, where the temperature averages 26.9°C.

Kamloops is one of the nicest spots on the planet, and if you love outdoor activities, this is your place. Name any sport or activity, and you'll find it in Kamloops: water sports, fishing, hunting, hiking, mountain climbing, biking, horseback riding; and in winter there's cross-country and downhill skiing in some of the best powder on the continent.

Maybe You Prefer Rainy Days?

The rainiest? Henderson Lake, BC, a fish hatchery on Vancouver Island and the wettest spot in North America

with an average recorded rainfall of 6650 millimetres. In 1997 they recorded 9082 millimetres, and while fish like it, the folks living there are prone to quoting from the Bible (Noah's story). All that rain, yet just 100 kilometres to the east over the Coast Mountains is the Fraser River Valley with some of the driest spots in Canada. Some sections of the Fraser River Valley receive only 250 millimetres of precipitation annually, a miniscule amount when compared to Henderson Lake.

Abbotsford, British Columbia, has the most rainy days, with an astounding yearly average of 171 rainy days. Close behind are St. John's and Vancouver with 162 and 161 rainy days. If you see an umbrella shop in your future, these are opening places.

Don't Like Rain?

Medicine Hat, Alberta, is the driest city in Canada with 270 (plus or minus a few) days without precipitation. Sounds too good to be true—there must be a catch. No catch; this is badlands country, with lots of sunshine and rainy days as rare as the dinosaur bones they find here. Great spot, lots of fun, and you can go bone picking and maybe find a *Tyrannosaurus rex*. They find them here and put them on display in their great museums, a must-see edifice of big bones. The badlands are weird, mostly hardscrabble desert eroded by winds into all kinds of fantastic formations, but that is where you'll find the dinosaurs. Dogs love it, but take along some treats, as they get frustrated digging up unchewable bones.

While the sun shines down on Medicine Hat, it's doing the same in Eureka, on Ellesmere Island, Nunavut, and while it rains sometimes in Medicine Hat, Eurekans get barely 60 millimetres per year, not enough to keep your potted violet alive for a week. Eureka is the driest spot in Canada—hung-up laundry dries in minutes, and if you like the cold, this is your spot. Winters here are over-the-top cold, with temps sometimes dipping to –50°C. Nice place to visit, but—well, you know. Canada is the coldest country on the planet, with an average temp of –5.6°C, and in places like Ellesmere Island, the average yearly temp is a bone snapping –19.9°C.

Prefer Snow?

If shovelling snow is your thing, Tahtsa Lake, BC, is your kind of place. It's the snowiest spot in Canada (978 centimetres per year) and holds the record for the deepest one-day snowfall—on April 8, 1999, a blizzard deposited 145 centimetres. Only four Canadian cities have seen more than a half metre fall in a single day: St. John's, Halifax, London and Victoria. I'll bet that last one is a surprise; it certainly was for Victoria residents unaccustomed to any snow, let alone the 150 centimetres that fell on December 29, 1996. To put that into perspective, that snowfall was only the seventh in Victoria's history. Not good if you like snow, because it might not fall again for decades, but Victoria is such a nice place you'll probably want to live there regardless.

Coldest Winters—Yellowknife, Northwest Territories, –28.9°C

Yellowknife, population 20,000, is a long way from anywhere and a city at the edge, a place where mining and logging companies get stuff. A wonderful town, with air so fresh it should be packaged and sold, and they got diamonds there, and long days of summer sunshine. But one morning (can it really be September?) you'll wake up searching for another blanket.

Winter has arrived, and it won't leave until May. Nice place, almost paradise on earth, but the winters are unbelievably cold. According to Environment Canada, Yellowknife holds more enviable and unenviable weather records than any other place in Canada: coldest winters, coldest spring, coldest year-round, most hot and cold days, longest snow cover season, most deep snow cover days, sunniest summer, sunniest spring, most heating degree days, extreme wind chill, most high wind chill days (−30°C or less), and driest winter air. If you're in a hurry to experience all of that, you can fly in from a lot of places, but if you have time on your hands and want to make some friends, Greyhound Bus Lines has a scheduled service from Edmonton.

Most Freezing Days—Thompson, Manitoba—240 days

Thompson, Manitoba, population 14,000, is another city on the edge where one mining company found a lot of good stuff. Inco discovered nickel there in 1956, built the town in 1957 and has ambitions to make the mine the largest producer of nickel in the world. Big business means plenty of cold cash and lots of fun-loving residents. Cold is fun in Thompson, with lots of snowmobiles, cross-country skiing, downhill skiing and ski planes. If you like winter sports, this is your spot, and for those 124 days when it's not freezing, they have a nine-hole golf course.

Fewest Freezing Days—Vancouver, BC—46 days

Ah, back into a warm climate. Vancouver is such a nice place, and you'll probably want to live there, but be warned, it takes a while to catch onto the dress code. It's a little chilly in the morning, so wear a sweater and jacket. By 10:00 AM, the jackets will be hanging off your arm, followed at noon by the sweater. Then an hour later it's pouring rain and you're looking for an umbrella shop. Don't worry, you'll soon get used to the quick weather changes and be wearing a nylon windbreaker, shorts and flip flops, just like the natives.

Least Sunshine Year-round—Prince Rupert, BC

Prince Rupert is a port town on British Columbia's north coast near the Alaskan border. It gets 1229 hours of sunshine per year and has the fewest sunny days year-round—250 days. Neat spot, and a place where anticipation reins—you will anticipate seeing grizzlies or whales, a boat or plane trip, arrival of the ferry, catching a salmon, eating the salmon, and rain. Not that it rains that much, it just always seems like it's going to start up cats and dogs at any moment.

Better take along your rain slicker, because when it does rain…it is cats and dogs.

Since weather going around comes around, you might want to keep these days in mind…

The Rainiest Day—Halifax, Nova Scotia

On August 15, 1971, Hurricane Beth dumped a massive 218 millimetres of rain. Flood damage was extensive; sections of roads and bridges washed out, power lines collapsed, but not one fatality. Halifax is neat, a big city on the Atlantic with plenty to do. But be warned, except during the summer months, you are liable to experience all four seasons in one day. It's like Vancouver, where what to wear in the morning is always a big problem. That aside, it's a real nice city, and if fresh air, lobsters and taking pictures of Peggy's Cove are your things, this is your spot.

The Hottest Day—Yellow Grass, Saskatchewan

On July 5, 1937, the mercury rose to an incredible, girder warping 45°C. That's hot, and if metrics is not your thing, think 113°F. The kids of Yellow Grass sold lots of lemonade on that day—whew!

Wheat is king in Yellow Grass, and you can still see grain elevators, but the place is tiny (population 2000), and there's not a lot to do unless you're into watching wheat grow or taking pics of grain elevators. But it's such a pretty spot, and housing is dirt cheap.

Significant Canadian Weather Events

Compared to other large countries, Canada appears to suffer fewer natural disasters. We have the odd flood, ice storm, drought, tornado and occasional errant hurricane, but nothing calamitous in terms of lives lost. Why is that? Are we better situated geographically? Better prepared? Or can it be our sparse population? If a tree falls in the forest and there is no one to hear, does it make a noise? An old bucket cliché, but it still holds water. Statistics Canada has us pegged at 3.2 people per square kilometre, while India, a country with disasters galore, weighs in at 330 people per square kilometre. A weather disaster is only that if it has an impact on people—no witnesses equals no disaster. This chapter contains a list of Canadian disasters that did have witnesses (courtesy of Environment Canada).

WEATHER DISASTERS

August 25, 1873—Nova Scotia and Newfoundland

They called it the Great Nova Scotia Cyclone, a hurricane that inflicted so much damage it became the impetus for Canadian government funding of a meteorological service. That insanely huge monster rolled up the eastern seaboard destroying over 1200 vessels, 1000 buildings and hundreds of bridges, dikes and wharves. In Nova Scotia it killed 500 people and caused many millions of dollars in property damage. Newfoundland also experienced the effects of this hurricane, with an additional 100 people killed from the storm's winds and flooding.

July 29, 1916—Northeastern Ontario

A violent thunderstorm rolled over the towns of Cochrane and Matheson and was initially thought heaven-sent as the surrounding forests had been bone dry for weeks. But the rain didn't last, and when the skies cleared, multiple plumes of smoke foretold a disaster. Lightning had started fires, lots of them, which eventually crowned and destroyed both towns, killing 233 people.

July 20, 1919—Biscotasing, Ontario

It was Ontario's hottest day, at 42.2°C. This northern Ontario logging community on the shores of Biscotasi Lake had no asphalt roads to melt, no metal girders to warp, and its mostly male residents suffered the day either immersed in the lake or drinking whiskey in icehouses. Bisco, as residents call it, is where the legendary Englishman, Archie Belaney, better known as Gray Owl, learned to hunt, trap, lie and drink whiskey.

July 6, 1921—Ville Marie, Québec

The mercury hit 40°C, the province's hottest recorded temperature. Most residents jumped into Lake Temiscamingue to cool off, while some probably took to the icehouses and drank beer and whiskey until the heat wave passed over.

July 12, 1926—Lac La Hache, British Columbia

A rare BC tornado struck Lac La Hache, destroying farm buildings and toppling thousands of trees.

July 5–17, 1936—Manitoba and Ontario

Canada's longest and deadliest heat wave claimed 1180 lives (mostly the elderly and infants). Temperatures in Manitoba and Ontario exceeded 44°C.

July 8–10, 1936—Toronto, Ontario

Temperatures soared to 40.6°C for two days. On July 10, it peaked at 41.1°C . Residents sought refuge at beaches, movie theatres with air conditioning and the countryside. But most had to tough it out, and 270 died from heat exhaustion. Record high temperatures for a city that had only two years earlier endured a winter with record low temps.

July 11, 1936—Atikokan, Ontario, and Winnipeg, Manitoba

The temperature peaked at 42.2°C in both communities. The Atikokan reading tied the highest temperature ever in Ontario.

July 11, 1936—St. Albans, Manitoba

Temperature reached a provincial record of 44.4°C, hot enough to melt the city's asphalt roads.

July 13, 1936—Fort Frances, Ontario

Temperature peaks at 42.2°C, tying the highest temperature ever in Ontario.

July 5, 1937—Yellow Grass, Saskatchewan

The mercury soared to 45°C, the highest temperature ever recorded in Canada.

July 16, 1941—Lillooet and Lytton, British Columbia

The day's high reached 44.4°C at both locations, the highest temperature ever reported in the province.

July 18, 1941—Fort Smith, Northwest Territories

Maximum temperature reached 39.4°C, the hottest ever reported in the territories.

July 4, 1944—Goose Bay, Labrador

Maximum temperature reaches 37.8°C.

June 27, 1946—Windsor, Ontario

A tornado roared across the Detroit River, killing 13 residents. Property damage was extensive and hundreds were injured.

February 3, 1947—Snag, Yukon

Snag recorded the lowest temperatures in Canadian history, at −62.8°C. Skies were clear, winds calm, visibility was unlimited, and 40 centimetres of snow lay on the ground.

July 7, 1949—St. John's, Newfoundland

The mercury soars at 30.6°C, the city's hottest day on record.

July 19, 1949—Cheneville, Québec

With a three-minute dash around town, a tornado demolished the small village of Cheneville.

July 1, 1962—Vancouver, British Columbia

A small tornado touched down near Vancouver, only the third such observation in the 33-year history of the Vancouver Weather Office.

July 10, 1973—Lethbridge, Alberta

The temperature soared to 39.4°C.

July 20, 1973—Arviat, Nunavut

Nunavut's hottest day, with a temperature of 33.9°C.

July 30, 1978—Yellowknife, Northwest Territories

A tornado, the third reported in the territory's previous 16 years, toppled a power transmission tower, skipped across the countryside and toppled another tower at Rae-Edzo.

July 31, 1987—Edmonton, Alberta

A massive tornado leaves 27 dead, 253 injured and hundreds homeless. Damage estimates exceeded $250 million.

July 2, 1991—Prince George, British Columbia

Severe thunderstorms spawn a small tornado at Clucluz Lake outside Prince George. In the city, hail and heavy rains hamper traffic. At the airport, 15.4 millimetres of rain fell in 25 minutes.

July 18, 1991—Pakwash Forest, Northwest Ontario

Approximately 1500 square kilometres of trees toppled by non-tornado winds in excess of 180 kilometres per hour. The damage path was roughly 20 kilometres wide and 75 kilometres long.

July 14, 1993—Windsor, Ontario

Humidex values at Windsor soared above 50°C, the highest ever reported in Canada to date.

July 18–21, 1996—Saguenay River Valley, Québec

Canada's first billion-dollar disaster occurred when deluge and flood triggered a surge of water, trees, rocks and mud that killed 10 and forced 12,000 residents to flee for their lives.

July 6–8, 1997—Southwest Coast, British Columbia

On July 6, more than 7000 lightning strikes in a 90-minute period lit up the skies over Greater Vancouver and southern

Vancouver Island. During the evening of July 7 and early morning of the 8th, Vancouver endured more than 37 millimetres of rain, the second heaviest one-day rainfall ever recorded in July. That total exceeded the normal rainfall for the entire month: 36 millimetres.

July 21, 1997—Okanagan, British Columbia

A hailstorm ripped through the orchards, making 40 percent of the fruit crop unsuitable for fresh markets and costing growers $100 million. Winds gusting to 100 kilometres per hour accompanied the rain, and hail capsized boats in the interior lakes and caused power outages and traffic accidents.

January 8, 1998—St. Lawrence River Valley, Ontario, and Québec

A warm, elongated low-pressure air mass moving up from the south and into the St. Lawrence River Valley wedged into a belt of cold arctic air and moved east while releasing water vapour. Super cooled by the frigid air underneath, the below-freezing rain stuck onto any cold surface and continued to build for five days. Canada's worst ice storm disaster affected millions of people, thousands of farms, destroyed whole forests and toppled a massive number of power transmission towers.

July 4, 1998—Calgary, Alberta

A record 43 millimetres of rain fell on the city in six hours, breaking the record set in 1909.

July 27, 1998—Osoyoos, British Columbia

Maximum temperature reached 42.8°C. Grape vines wilted, and Canada's warmest lake, Lake Osoyoos, got even warmer.

July 15, 1999—Calgary, Alberta

Temperatures plunged to a chilling –2.7°C, and residents foolish enough to keep their picnic and beach appointments braved snow flurries and winds gusting to 69 kilometres per hour.

July 3, 2000—Vanguard, Saskatchewan

Severe thunderstorms deluged Vanguard with 375 millimetres of rain in eight hours, the greatest eight-hour rainfall ever recorded on the Prairies.

July 14, 2000—Pine Lake, Alberta

An F3 tornado chewed up cottages, docks, marinas and a trailer park, leaving 12 dead and 140 injured.

July 1, 2001—Kapuskasing, Ontario

Three centimetres of snow fell on the town's Canada Day celebration, probably causing a tow truck to receive the Best Float Award.

July 8, 2003—Ste-Jeanne-d'Arc, Québec

A weak tornado swirled across a farm near Ste-Jeanne-d'Arc, splitting trees and lifting several buildings off their foundations.

July 9, 2004—Grande Prairie, Alberta

A tornado swept through Grande Prairie, about 450 kilometres northwest of Edmonton. No injuries were reported, but a car flipped, hydro poles snapped and shingles were ripped from buildings.

July 11, 2004—Edmonton, Alberta

A severe summer storm soaks the city and suburbs with 200 millimetres of rain and damaging hail that piled up one metre high in the streets. The punishing rain and golf ball–sized hailstones caused millions of dollars in damage to the city's famous West Edmonton Mall. Tornadoes and funnel clouds were reported in rural areas around the city.

July 15, 2004—Peterborough, Ontario

An intense thunderstorm deluged the Peterborough area in the early-morning hours. Official rainfall totals ranged from

100 millimetres at the airport to 240 millimetres at Trent University, with most of the accumulation falling in less than five hours.

July 21, 2004—Durham-Sud, Québec

A strong tornado zigzags through Durham-Sud, damaging cars and houses and ripping roofs off buildings.

July 21–23, 2004—British Columbia

Extreme heat settles across the province, breaking 63 maximum temperature records from Vancouver Island to Fort St. John. Cats abandoned roofs all over BC, and in Lytton, the temp reached a sweltering 42°C for two days, making it the provincial hot spot.

July 23, 2004—Victoria, British Columbia

The day's high reached 35.3°C at Victoria's Gonzales Heights Observatory, the hottest day in the 100-year record at that climate station.

July 14, 2006—Gretna, Manitoba

A tornado pounced on Gretna, levelling fields of crops, blowing down barns, sheds, garages, hydro poles, and uprooting dozens of trees, some close to one metre in diameter.

July 21, 2006—New Brunswick and Nova Scotia

Remains of tropical storm Beryl soak southern New Brunswick and Nova Scotia. Storm rainfall totalled more than 60 millimetres around Fredericton, New Brunswick, while strong wind gusts exceeded 96 kilometres per hour on the southwestern tip of Nova Scotia.

July 10, 2007—Argyle Shore, Prince Edward Island

A waterspout is spotted off Argyle Shore, a hardly noteworthy event, but soon made so by the appearance of a dozen more spouts. Holiday beach goers were treated to a passing parade of waterspouts, an amazing, once-in-a-lifetime atmospheric spectacle.

July 24, 2007—Coronach and Rockglen, Saskatchewan

The afternoon temperature soared to 42°C, and an automate weather station at Rockglen, Saskatchewan, hit an unofficial high of 46°C. Had that reading been official, it would have exceeded Canada's highest temperature ever: 113°C, set on July 5, 1937. Coronach and Rockglen are small towns nestled in the Burning Hills of the Wood Mountain area, hills that really lived up to their name on that day.

Weather Phenomena

Woe unto the inhabitants of the seacoast.

–Zephaniah 2:5

HURRICANES

The Big Blow

It's strange that people are not more afraid of hurricanes. A tourist destination will take an awful thrashing, and when the next hurricane comes along, residents and tourists are back to waiting out the ordeal at hurricane parties. These folks have short memories, and usually of Category 0–2 hurricanes, with winds gusting from 119 to 177 kilometres per hour.

Categories 3–5, with winds of 178 to 250 kilometres per hour, are a whole other ball game and akin to being on the sidelines of a thermonuclear explosion. Canada is too far north to experience many big blows, but we do get tail ends and have had some rippers. In 1954, Ontario and Québec got the remnants of a Category 4 monster called Hazel and suffered massive flooding and the deaths of 81 people. And while the actual landfall of Category hurricanes onto Canadian soil is rare, there have been a few.

Way back in 1775, a cyclone dubbed the Newfoundland Hurricane struck the Grand Banks wiping it clean of sailing vessels and drowning over 4000 sailors, including the crew of two British war ships. That was one of the deadliest Atlantic hurricanes of all time and the worst natural disaster in Canadian history (Newfoundland included, because a Canada without is unimaginable).

The worst Atlantic hurricane occurred only five years later and killed over 25,000 people. Dubbed the Great Hurricane, that Category 5 blow smashed Caribbean islands and roared up the eastern seaboard where it decimated American and British fleets engaged in fighting the American War of Independence. Newfoundland got the tail end of that wind before the hurricane disappeared into the North Atlantic.

After that Great One, Canada's east coast saw only dissipating tail enders (called gales) until just after midnight on September 29, 2003, when along came Juan, a non-dissipating Category 2 ripper that crashed through Nova Scotia like a runaway cement truck. Why did it maintain wind speed all the way from the Caribbean and fail to dissipate? The answer is—warm water, as luck would have it, the seas below and around Nova Scotia were unseasonably warm, enabling Juan to keep on truckin'. It made landfall with sustained winds of 151 kilometres per hour, knocking down forests, hydro poles, bridges, buildings, and dumping enormous quantities of rainwater on Nova Scotia. Juan was so devastating to Nova Scotia that the government asked for the name to be retired, but a few years later, on February 18, 2004, along comes a ripper snow storm that newspapers affectionately dubbed…White Juan. Time heals all, and eventually there will be a…Wet Juan.

Birth of a Hurricane

North American hurricanes usually rise from between 5 and 25 degrees north and south latitude, in an area of warm surface water off the west coast of Africa. Constant evaporation of this surface water creates enormous amounts of heat and energy that rises up in huge columns of low pressure. Aloft and into cooler air, these columns quickly condense back into water, releasing vast amounts of energy. Cumulonimbus clouds blot the horizon, lightning flashes constantly, and rain falls so hard that day turns to night. Thunderstorms, but on a vast scale, and every year a few hundred of these tropical giants form and dissipate. Only a dozen or so will encounter conditions favouring the spiral movement of a hurricane. Warm surface water (26°C) over a large expanse of ocean combines with cool air aloft to permit rapid condensation. If conditions are perfect, wet air is pumped up from the surface of the ocean at a faster and faster rate creating ever-stronger Coriolis-affected circulating winds, the dreaded spiral. When circulating winds reach speeds of 64 kilometres per hour, the storm is designated a tropical storm by the National Hurricane Center in the U.S., given a name and assigned a category on a five-point hurricane scale.

Saffir-Simpson Hurricane Scale

- **Category 1—winds 119 to 153 kilometres per hour**
  No real damage to buildings. Damage to unanchored mobile homes. Some damage to poorly constructed signs and some coastal flooding and minor pier damage. Examples: Irene 1999 and Allison 1995.

- **Category 2—winds 154 to 177 kilometres per hour**
  Damage to building roofs, doors, windows and mobile homes. Flooding damages piers and small craft in unprotected moorings may break their moorings. A few trees blown down and shingles ripped off roofs. Examples: Bonnie 1998, George (Florida and Los Angeles) 1998 and Gloria 1985.

- **Category 3—winds 178 to 209 kilometres per hour**
  Structural damage to small residences and utility buildings. Large trees blown down, mobile homes and poorly built signs destroyed. Flooding near the coast destroys smaller structures, with larger structures damaged by floating debris. Terrain may be flooded well inland. Examples: Keith 2000, Fran 1996, Opal 1995, Alicia 1983 and Betsy 1965.

- **Category 4—winds 210 to 249 kilometres per hour**
  Complete roof structure failure on small residences. Major erosion of beach areas and flooding inland. Examples: Hugo 1989 and Donna 1960.

- **Category 5—winds 250+ kilometres per hour**
  Complete roof failure on many residences and industrial buildings. Some complete building failures with small utility structures blown over or away. Flooding of coastal areas may require massive evacuation of residential areas. Examples: Andrew (Florida) 1992, Camille 1969 and Labour Day 1935.

FLOODS

Water, Water, Everywhere

Lions going out like lambs in March is a springtime adage that absolutely terrifies Canadian insurance companies. In their minds, the adage is reversed, and March goes out like a ferocious lion, causing millions of dollars in flood damage. Floods are by far Canada's most expensive natural disasters, and they can happen anywhere at anytime.

Canada's first recorded major flood occurred in 1826, at Fort Garry, a Hudson Bay outpost on the banks of the Red River and the place where Lord Selkirk sent his Scottish and Irish settlers in 1811.

Starting on May 3, 1826, and reacting to an early thaw and ice jam, the Red River rose 2.7 metres in 24 hours and completely inundated Fort Garry. In later years, that 2.7-metre rise got pegged by insurance actuators as a once-in-667-year event and became the benchmark of Red River flooding. Flooding is normal for the Red and Assiniboine rivers, especially the former, which, along with Lake Winnipeg, owes its existence to the last Quaternary period ice sheet. The ice retreated 10,000 years ago, leaving the Red River Valley pancake flat with a shallow river channel. This was bad luck for early settlers, who built Fort Garry in spite of repeated warnings from local First Nation peoples who knew from experience not to trust the Red River.

Hudson Bay Company post factors (managers) were required to keep a log of noteworthy events that were later entered into the company's *Journal of Occurrences*. Fort Garry's post factor logged the following events during the great flood of 1826.

May 3—Water underneath the ice has raised it to the level of the spring flood of the previous year. The weather was cold and the rain kept up all day.

May 4—The river rose four feet. A mixture of rain, sleet and snow added to the dampness.

May 5—The ice broke up and the water slopped over the riverbanks. It started as a trickle, but soon swelled to flood proportions, carrying away cattle, houses, and fences. A total of 47 dwellings were lifted from their foundations and swirled downstream within half an hour.

May 6—The weather became warmer and there was a rumble of thunder and rain showers.

May 7—Still raining. The ice went out on the Assiniboine River. Company employees using company boats were busy helping settlers to higher ground and moving their stock and effects.

May 10—Started to storm with thunder and lightning and a torrential downpour of rain.

May 14—Most of the settlers had either moved or were moving to high ground near Sturgeon Creek (north of Grant Town, Cuthbert Grants Métis settlement, near what is now Little Mountain Park). Settlers on the east bank fled to Pine Hill (now referred to as Birds Hill) and to a settlement then known as Roseneath.

May 17—The water still rising, two-foot rise in 24 hours.

May 20—Another gale from the northwest lashed the floodwater to a sullen anger and relentlessly the water continued to climb.

May 23—The water's level declined two inches.

June 25—The Hudson's Bay Co. people returned to the fort to find complete ruin. Hordes of mosquitoes made life miserable.

During the summer of 1826, some 250 settlers left the area, mainly members discharged from the Regiment des Meurons.

July 2—Almost all of the floodwater was now contained within the riverbanks and the settlers were starting to rebuild.

Here is another eyewitness account of the 1826 flood (from the archives of Environment Canada):

"While the frightened inhabitants were collected into groups on any dry spot that remained visible above the waste of waters, their houses, barns, carriages, furniture, fencing and every description of property might be seen floating along over the wide extended plain, to be engulfed in Lake Winnipeg."

Major flooding of the Red River occurred again in 1852, causing 75 percent of the population to abandon the settlement at Fort Garry and move to Lower Fort Garry, near what is now the city of Selkirk, Manitoba. Then a most amazing thing happened. The river did nothing for almost a century, and in that time the city of Winnipeg grew out of the Red and Assiniboine river settlements and thrived on the prairie grain trade. Then in 1950 the river stopped being nice and flooded a quarter of the city, driving 100,000 people from their homes. The 1950 Red River flood caused damage in excess of $1 billion (2009 value) and remains one of Canada's most expensive natural disasters. Nationally, floods cause many millions in damage and claim many lives.

Hey, Martha! Why does this guy think we should we be interested in floods?

What happened in Winnipeg could happen in your town. All it takes are the right conditions: ground saturated from a previous rainfall, a late spring thaw or heavy snow cover, and a deluge. Winnipeg has spent a fortune on flood control and it's working, but maybe your town fathers are thinking it can't happen here, because it never has before.

Southern Québec has many rivers, and most are robust with substantial rocky banks and deep channels. "Our rivers can handle anything nature throws our way," was the general mindset of the population. That soon changed, when from July 18 to 21, 1996, a major storm system stalled over the St. Lawrence River, dropping more than 200 millimetres of rain on an already saturated mountainous area south of the Jonquiere-Chicoutimi region of the Saguenay Valley. Unable to absorb any water because of previous rainfalls, the mountains funnelled rain into the waterways feeding the robust Saguenay River. Overwhelmed, both the feeder streams and Saguenay River suffered major overflows resulting in the evacuation of 12,000 people and the loss of over 1000 homes. It was another "who would have thought it could happen here event," and if you live near a stream or river, better keep in mind it could happen to you. A sudden overabundance of rainwater onto already saturated soil can turn the most benign stream into a house-eating monster.

Floods are nature's surprise party for Canadians who like rain. How about a month of rain in one day?

We've already covered Saguenay, Québec, where nobody could have predicted a tropical monsoon for the area; a split in the jet stream over the St. Lawrence pulled in a long mass of warm, wet air from the Caribbean and slammed it against a stationary arctic cold front. A prelude to the 1998 Great Ice Storm, it created the same pipeline effect and dumped tons of water down mountainsides into rivers that quickly overran their banks.

If you live near rivers or streams, be prepared for flash floods. Be alert for heavy, upstream rainfall, or you could be in for a watery surprise. If you receive evacuation orders, obey them, and never attempt to cross roadways covered with water. Flood currents are always stronger than they appear, and they will sweep you off your feet.

Make a list of things that you will need and can find quickly in case of emergency evacuation. Get adequate insurance, and if you already have a home policy, make sure there is flood coverage. Canadian property insurers can be tricky when it comes to act of God events, and river and stream overflow is not normal coverage in a standard policy.

Here is a valuable checklist of things to do before, during and after a flood.

Before a Flood

- Make sure any photos or videos of all of your important possessions are in a safe place. These documents will help you file a full flood insurance claim.

- Store important documents and irreplaceable personal objects (such as photographs) in a place where they won't be damaged.

- Move furniture and valuables to the upper levels of your home.

- Make sure your sump pump is working.

- Clear away debris from gutters and downspouts.

- Buy and install sump pumps with back-up power.

- Anchor fuel tanks. An unanchored tank in your basement can be torn free by floodwaters, and the broken supply line can contaminate your basement. An unanchored tank outside can be swept downstream, where it can damage other houses.

- Have a licensed electrician raise electric components (switches, sockets, circuit breakers and wiring) at least 30 centimetres above your home's projected flood elevation.

- Place the furnace and water heater on masonry blocks or concrete at least 30 centimetres above the projected flood elevation.

- If your washer and dryer are in the basement, elevate them on masonry or pressure-treated lumber at least 30 centimetres above the projected flood elevation.

- Have a family emergency plan: post emergency telephone numbers by the phone. Teach children to dial 911. Plan and practice a flood-evacuation route with your family. Ask an out-of-province relative or friend to be the "family contact" in case your family is separated during a flood. Make sure everyone in your family knows the name, address and phone number of this contact person.

- Don't forget to have a plan for your pets.

During a Flood

- Fill bathtubs, sinks and jugs with clean water in case water becomes contaminated.

- Listen to a battery-operated radio for the latest storm information.

- If local authorities instruct you to do so, turn off all utilities at the main power switch and close the main gas valve.

- If told to evacuate your home, do so immediately.

- If water rises inside your house before you have evacuated, retreat to the second floor, the attic, and if necessary the roof, and wait for assistance.

- Floodwaters may carry raw sewage, chemical waste and other disease-spreading substances. If you've come in contact with floodwaters, wash your hands with soap and disinfected water.

- Avoid walking through floodwaters. As little as 15 centimetres of moving water can knock you off your feet.

- Don't drive through a flooded area. If you come upon a flooded road, turn around and go another way. A car can be carried away by just 60 centimetres of floodwater.

- Electric current passes easily through water, so stay away from downed power lines and electrical wires.

- Look out for animals—especially snakes. Animals lose their homes in floods, too.

After a Flood

- If your home has suffered damage, call the agent who handles your flood insurance to file a claim. If you are unable to stay in your home, make sure to say where you can be reached.

- Take photos of any water in the house, and save damaged personal property. This will make filing your claim easier. If necessary, place these items outside the home. An insurance adjuster will need to see what's been damaged in order to process your claim.

- Check for structural damage before re-entering your home. Don't go inside if there is a chance of the building collapsing.

- Do not use matches, cigarette lighters or other open flames upon re-entering your property. Gas may be trapped inside. If you smell gas or hear hissing, open a window, leave quickly and call the gas company from a neighbour's home.

- Keep power off until an electrician has inspected your system for safety.

- Avoid using the toilets and the taps until you have checked for sewage and water line damage. If you suspect damage, call a plumber.

- Throw away any food, including canned goods, that has come in contact with floodwaters.

- Boil water for drinking and food preparation until local authorities declare your water supply to be safe.

- Salvage water-damaged books, heirlooms and photographs.

- Follow local building codes and ordinances when rebuilding. Use flood-resistant materials and techniques to protect your property from future flood damage.

Source: National Flood Insurance Program (U.S.)

TSUNAMI

Making Waves

"Tsunami" is the Japanese word for "tidal wave," a non-weather phenomenon caused by earthquakes, and is only included here because if weather conditions are bad at the time of occurrence, the results can be catastrophic.

On November 18, 1929, an earthquake ripped through Newfoundland's Grand Banks, displacing a huge section of the Laurentian slope seabed. This undersea land slump raised up three tsunamis (pulses) that wiped clean a 50-kilometre section of shoreline. Hardest hit was the Burin Peninsula, where the narrowing topography caused one of the pulses to rise over 13 metres, smashing the community of Lord's Cove. Here is an excerpt from the November 27, 1929, account from Honourable Dr. Mosdell aboard the *Meigle*, as reported in St. John's *The Daily News:*

Dwelling houses were reduced to a condition reminiscent of wartime description of the effects of heavy shell fire....Motor boats, stages and wharfs piers lifted bodily and thrown far inland in heaps of ruins. Lord's Cove and Lamaline visited by the relief expedition yesterday here dozen of houses, stores and stages were found thrown bodily into the pond at the head of the harbours, huddled together in one heap of destruction. Some lay upright but half submerged while others lay on their sides, and still others were entirely overturned.

That last and biggest wave killed 27 residents of Lord's Cove and decimated the community. But it got worse; the next morning a winter blizzard arrived, making it impossible to get out word of the disaster. The survivors huddled alone and afraid for three days before help arrived.

On Good Friday, March 27, 1964, Anchorage, Alaska, was rocked by one of the strongest earthquakes of the century. Measuring 8.5 on the Richter scale, the quake raised a section of the ocean floor by 15 metres causing a tsunami to travel out from the Gulf of Alaska where it reached speeds of 720 kilometres per hour.

At midnight, 4½ hours after the earthquake, the first of these waves reached Vancouver Island and entered the mouth of Alberni Inlet. As the waves entered the funnel-shaped inlet, the narrowing shoreline forced the waves to pile up. It travelled the 60 kilometres to Port Alberni in 10 minutes (360 kilometres per hour) and inundated half the town.

The second wave was the most damaging, cresting three metres above the high-tide mark as it raced inland and into the homes of sleeping residents. Four less forceful waves stormed in between 3:00 AM and 6:45 AM, reaching levels about two metres above the high-tide mark.

In all, 58 properties were destroyed, 350 buildings damaged and 300 vehicles written off, but luckily, nobody was drowned or seriously injured, and fair weather enabled the situation to be spotted from the air. Help arrived in hours that might have been days had the weather been foul.

AVALANCHES

Snowed Under

Snow falls from high altitudes, and while every flake is different, some are more different than others depending on temperature at those altitudes. In 1954, a Japanese scientist named Ukichiro Nakaya succeeded in growing snow crystals on a rabbit's hair and discovered their infinite shapes could be categorized into seven types depending on temperature and vapour count at altitude.

How does Nakaya's discovery benefit avalanche specialists? Well, if they can identify the basic type of snowflake on the ground, they can read the conditions in the clouds above. Nakaya called his discovery "letters from the sky," because they brought along that information.

Here is the list of the seven types of snow crystals that Nakaya categorized:

Temperature °C	Ice Crystal Type
0 to –3	Thin hexagonal plates
–3 to –5	Needles
–5 to –8	Hollow prismatic columns
–8 to –12	Hexagonal plates
–12 to –16	Dendrite, fern-like crystals
–16 to –25	Hexagonal plates
–25 to –50	Hollow prisms

Snow builds up in layers and degenerates into something called old snow—new flakes falling onto old and fusing together to form a solid mass. There are three kinds of old snow: wet, dry and slab, with dry (or powder) being the most common. A heavy fall of dry powder will fail to bind to the preceding layer and becomes unstable. A grave threat to skiers, but nevertheless readable in that it looks big, fluffy and able to move at the slightest provocation. Not so readable are the wet and slab varieties. The snow looks fine and well travelled, but then, for no particular reason, it suddenly begins to move in one great chunk.

What happened? Nakaya's list happened; the old snow had layers of different crystal types, sunshine warmed the mass, the layers became unbound, and the entire slope sheared off at the weakest layer. In wet snow that might be a layer of ice, but with slab, it can be any layer, and whole mountainsides have come unglued.

Skiers should be leery of sunshine on expansive snow cover and make frequent stops to reconnoitre. If the snow looks even the tiniest bit suspicious, turn around slowly and follow your ski tracks back to a safe area. The Rogers Pass area in southeastern British Columbia is a good example of the hazardous nature of avalanches. In 1881 the only barrier blocking east and west confederation of Canada were the Selkirk Mountains, and in that year the Canadian Pacific Railway Company appointed Major A.B. Rogers to push a rail line through to the coast. It took Rogers 30 years, and avalanches cost the lives of over 250 CPR employees—62 killed in a single event. Avalanches were so numerous that in 1912, CPR began the four-year construction of the Connaught Tunnel through the mountains to minimize the danger to trains.

That worked for trains, but people still die. On February 1, 2003, seven students from an Alberta high school were overrun and killed while on a field trip to study avalanches. A sad affair, which hopefully will serve as a warning to others wanting to tread in dangerous places.

LANDSLIDES

Look Out Below!

Many things may cause sediment to lose adhesion and slip, but in Canada, it's mainly deluge, and it can happen to any hill or mountain, and in any province. Landslides kill a lot of people, and mostly in British Columbia. Makes you wonder why.

Hey, Martha! This place has a great view. Let's build our house here.

People will build in dangerous places and for all kinds of reasons. Martha's hubby likes the view; some like isolation and clean air, while others build because jobs are there. In 1901, coal was discovered in a limestone behemoth called Turtle Mountain not far from Calgary, Alberta. First Nation peoples wouldn't go near the place and called it "the mountain that walks."

Turtle Mountain did move, a fact that delighted the mine owners who immediately sank shafts into the mountain and opened huge rooms called stopes. They didn't have to blast, because almost every day the mountain trembled and shook loose tons of coal from the stopes. Miners simply shovelled it up into coal trolleys. A good job, and by 1903, the small town of Frank lay in the shadow of the mountain that moved. First Nation peoples thought those residents a bit touched by spirits, and you have to marvel at the miners' gullibility for believing that mine was safe. Maybe the owners only hired touched people? We'll never know, because very early (4:00 AM) on April 29, 1903, 100 million tons of limestone fell onto the little community of Frank. The official death toll was 76, but was probably much higher as the town's population consisted of itinerant mine and railway workers with no families to report them missing.

Alberta is not the only place in Canada where mountains walk; British Columbia has some that almost jump and dance around. Landslides account for more loss of life and property damage in British Columbia than any other natural hazard. In January 1965, that province saw a redux of the Frank slide when the southeast slope of Johnston Peak collapsed. Falling debris from Johnston Peak buried a three-kilometre stretch of the Hope-Princeton Highway under 85 metres of rubble and completely obliterated Outram Lake located in the valley below. Luckily, it was off-season, and the sparsely populated area suffered only four fatalities.

The St. Lawrence Valley is another area of Canada prone to landslides and one of the most active on the planet. When the last glacier departed this area around 13,000 years ago, the sea flooded in to create a body of water called the Champlain Sea. Eventually drained by the St. Lawrence River, the sea left behind clay sediment called Leda Clay that is prone to

slippage from uplifting topography. But a deluge can turn the stuff into a brown soup and send it off just as easily. Called retrogressive flowslides, this fluidized clay can sometimes block rivers and cause flooding. Flowslide-caused floods are common in Québec, and since 1840 have caused over 100 fatalities. In 1971, at St. Jean-Vianney, Québec, a large, rapid retrogressive flowslide carried 40 homes to destruction and took the lives of 31 people.

Big rock slides such as those in Frank and Hope cause immense damage but happen infrequently; it's the smaller slides that empty provincial coffers. In 1991, a very small landslide near Logger's Creek, north of Vancouver, damaged a major highway and cost $7 million to clear and repair. While on May 27, 2008, a rockslide closed Highway 97, a major north-south freeway running through BC's Okanagan Valley and used by 14,000 vehicles daily. At this writing, the road is almost clear of debris, and cost estimates are around $15 million.

Rockslides and falls are expensive and occur frequently in Canada, and there's not a lot to be done except to pick up the mess. Local governments shore up one area and rocks fall from another, and it's not the job of building inspectors to check outcrops of rotten rock looming over new houses.

GRAUPEL

Not-so-nice Ice

This funny word comes from the German but means the same everywhere: ships sinking, planes crashing, cars colliding and skiers caught in avalanches. Graupel are ice pellets that form when water droplets collide and adhere to snowflakes, turning them into tiny ball bearings that stick like glue to any cold object.

The sticking is called rime ice and can be extremely dangerous. We have all seen pictures of sailors chopping ice from ships, that is rime ice, and the look of desperation on the sailors' faces is there because if they don't chop fast enough, their ship will turn turtle and sink. Rime ice has capsized hundreds of ships and downed many airplanes. It topples power transmission poles, light standards, docks, piers, anything cold. What it does to roads and mountainsides is different but equally insidious.

Graupel is usually a transient phenomenon caused by a temporary wind shear. It's over quickly, but enough can fall to cover almost everything with a thin sheet of icy ball bearings. Vehicles slide off roads, and on mountainsides, snow falling onto graupel builds onto an extremely unstable surface.

HAIL

Ice From Above

Born in super cell clouds, these rocks of ice can lambaste the ground like mortar shells and cause extensive damage to crops, livestock, homes, vehicles and dog walkers. Hailstones are raindrops caught in the updraft of a super cell altocumulus cloud. The draft keeps pushing the drops higher and higher until they freeze. Now an ice pellet and heavy, the frozen drops fall while attracting more water droplets. But often they're caught up again in the clouds strengthening updraft and go up again. Up and down like a yoyo, and each time, the water droplets become coated with more water until finally they are just too heavy to shoot up and fall to earth.

How many times can a water droplet yo-yo? Nobody knows, but the unofficial record weight for a hailstone is one kilogram, a monster that fell with many others on April 14, 1986, in Bangladesh, killing 96 people and more than 2000 cows.

The heaviest officially recorded hailstone fell on Coffeyville, Kansas, on September 3, 1970, and weighed a hefty 766 grams, while the largest officially measured hailstone pounded onto the ground in south-central Nebraska in June 2003. About the size of a soccer ball (17.8 centimetres), that chunk of ice got thrown into a freezer and is now preserved for posterity by the National Centre for Atmospheric Research in Boulder, Colorado.

The largest, officially recorded hailstone in Canada was 290 grams (think grapefruit), and it fell on Cedoux, Saskatchewan, in August 1973. On July 14, 1953, a hailstorm pelted southern Alberta's prairie land with golf ball–sized stones carving out a swatch of destruction eight kilometres wide and 225 kilometres long. The huge stones turned cows into hamburger, obliterated crops and killed an estimated 36,000 birds. Bad got even worse, when four days later, as if to add insult to injury, another hailstorm worked over the same area, killing a further 27,000 birds.

But the absolute worst occurred a few decades later on September 7, 1991, when the granddaddy of Canadian hailstorms overran Calgary, Alberta, causing half a billion dollars in damage. Car dealerships saw their stock dented beyond repair, windows broken everywhere, countless roofs mangled, trees split, thousands of birds killed, and the bombardment continued for 30 minutes.

A few years later, in 1996, both Calgary and Winnipeg got bombarded with stones the size of oranges. The huge stones smashed everything and plugged the city's drainage systems, causing flood damage. As if that wasn't bad enough, six days later another hailstorm worked over Calgary, smashing up whatever the first one had missed.

Alberta and our Prairie provinces are hailstorm central; they suffer more icy bombardments than any place on the planet and lose three percent of their crops to the phenomena.

Small hailstones are cone shaped, larger ones are round, and the real biggies are oval and covered with icy protrusions caused by water spinning off as they fall to earth. Most hailstones are small, like peas, but enough walnut-sized stones fall onto Canadian farms to cause extensive damage to crops. Hail damage to food crops affects all Canadians: groceries cost more, insurance premiums rise, and many farmers quit the land.

What to Do in a Hailstorm

- Always have a battery-operated radio handy to listen to updates on the hailstorm activity in your area.

- Stay indoors no matter what personal property is outside.

- If the hailstorm has not hit, try to put your vehicle in a garage to protect it from damage.

- If you are in a vehicle, pull over to the side of the road and try to get underneath an overpass to shield the vehicle from the hail.

- Tornadoes may cause hail, so keep your eyes peeled, listen for the freight train noise, and be prepared to find cover fast.

FOG

Serving Up Some Pea Soup

The province of Newfoundland and Labrador is the foggiest place on the planet, with some seaside communities subjected to an average 200 pea soup days per year. "Pea soup" is a British idiom once reserved for a thick, yellow fog that tasted of sulphur, a noxious blanket of poisoned air once common to European cities that burned soft coal.

On December 5, 1952, a cold fog descended on London, England, and folks lit up a million or so coal fires. Trapped by a cold-air temperature inversion, smoke from those fires piled up to such an extent that the elderly, newborns and people with respiratory problems died. It lasted five days and killed 4000 citizens, with 8000 more dying in the weeks following. A major catastrophe, but it led to a good thing, the passing of Britain's 1956 Clean Air Act and the outlawing of coal-burning fireplaces.

Argentia, Newfoundland, suffers more foggy days than any place on Earth, with an average 206 days of pea soup. It's a nice place to visit with magnificent scenery, but for two-thirds of your stay you won't see a thing. How come? It's because the sea around Argentia is cold, and warm air masses moving over them are cooled and lose water vapour through condensation. If there is no wind or breeze to move and coalesce the drops into rain, they will hang in the air, reducing visibility. This is called advection fog and occurs mostly in the spring and summer months. In areas of the Grand Banks, advection fog can be extremely heavy, long-lived and worrisome to ships at sea.

When a reverse process occurs, cool air moving over warm seas, the resulting fog, called sea smoke, is caused by evaporation condensing back into water droplets. Sea smoke is most common in arctic areas during ice break-ups when cold air blows over open patches of warm water. This is also what cause lake effect snowstorms on large bodies of fresh water.

Advection fog and sea smoke are both common to the St. Lawrence River during early spring when a warmer flow encounters cold water from the Atlantic and seasonal atmospheric conditions. On May 29, 1914, in a particularly dense combination fog, Canadian Pacific's luxury liner *Empress of Ireland* was proceeding down river towards Montréal and was struck amidships by a Norwegian vessel heavily laden with coal. Frantic signals from the *Empress* for the Norwegian ship to stay put and keep the hole plugged went unanswered. The Norwegian ship pulled away, and the *Empress* sank in 14 minutes, not enough time to get passengers awake and into lifeboats. Fatalities numbered 1014, making it Canada's worst ever weather-related disaster.

Inland fog is normally caused by heat radiating from the ground on cloudless nights and is called radiation fog, or ground fog, and is usually dissipated by morning sunshine. Warm fronts may cause fog when rising over saturated cooler air; fog can also occur in very cold air, usually arctic air. Cold, arctic air holds very little moisture, and when cooled further, that little moisture condenses out as ice crystals.

Fog costs Canadian companies millions of dollars every year. It causes shipping delays, offshore oil rigs to close down for the duration, and spectacular car crashes on busy highways. Fog is dangerous and can be calamitous. At the Canary Islands airport in 1977, two Boeing 747s collided on the runway in a pea soup fog, and 582 people perished, making it the world's worst aviation disaster.

ICE STORMS

A Canadian Catastrophe

Canada sees a lot of freezing rain when El Niño prowls the Pacific during winter. This huge low causes air to move around the Americas in a counter-clockwise motion, pulling cold from our north and pushing around warm, moist air. When the circle is complete, the warm air mass rises into the cold like a wedge forming an icy sandwich with a warm air filling. Cooled by proximity, water vapour in the upper parts of the sandwich filling coalesce into snowflakes that fall through the warm layer and melt. Icy rain enters the cold bottom section and is supercooled before striking the ground. Normally this is simply an inconvenience to drivers because both air masses are rapidly heading west: slippery roads, some wires down, nothing we can't handle. Problems only arise when the circle slows or stalls in close proximity to a moving arctic air mass, and tropical air piles so high it creates a bulge in the higher atmospheres causing an anomaly that can split a jet stream. That is what occurred during the first few days of January in 1998, when a split in a U.S. subtropical jet stream pulled a narrow band of moist, warm air from the Caribbean and pushed it north and into the St. Lawrence River Valley. That warm, wet air wedged into a descending arctic air mass and became a pipeline to the Caribbean.

From January 5 to 10, 1998, precipitation, composed mostly of freezing rain and ice pellets, exceeded 85 millimetres in Ottawa, 73 millimetres in Kingston, 108 millimetres in Cornwall and 100 millimetres in Montréal. According to Environment Canada, the length of the storm caused Canada's most expensive natural disaster. Six days of unrelenting icy precipitation fell onto a vast area coating everything with a thick layer of ice. At the peak of the storm, the area of freezing precipitation extended from central Ontario through eastern Ontario, western Québec and the Eastern Townships to New Brunswick and Nova Scotia. In the United States, ice coated northern New York and parts of New England. Electric power was disrupted in all those areas, and three weeks after the event, 700,000 homes were still without electricity. Total fatalities from acute hypothermia were at least 25, while many other succumbed to heart attacks or just gave up living in the cold and darkness.

In Ontario, 100,000 homes lost power, while in Québec the number was astounding, affecting over 900,000 households. Air and rail travel shut down, while some local roads in disaster areas stayed closed for weeks. Millions of residents were forced into either communal living or a gypsy existence of visiting friends or relatives for a shower, shave or hot meal. Millions of trees were toppled or damaged, 120,000 kilometres of power lines came down, along with 130 major power transmission towers and 30,000 wooden poles. The entire electrical grid had to be rebuilt, and volunteer electrical workers arrived from all over to help: linesmen from across Canada and the U.S. were there for weeks. Ontario Hydro linesmen working around the clock and ordered to take breaks refused, saying every minute they worked another victim would see light. When power was restored to an area, its residents would troop out to applaud their heroes and present hot soup and coffee from their now operating stoves.

Nothing makes heroes like weather disasters, and after January 10, Canada had them by the hundreds. Why our government has not created medals for those guys is a mystery.

Tornadoes

The Fujita scale—developed in 1971 by T. Theodore Fujita of the University of Chicago—measures the damage to human-made structures to rate the intensity of a tornado. Wind speeds are based on estimates. Only one percent of all tornadoes reach the Fujita-scale class of F4–F5. Seventy-four percent of tornadoes are F0–F1, and 25 percent are F2–F3. Sixty-seven percent of tornado-related deaths occur during F4–F5 storms; 29 percent during F2–F3 tornadoes.

ATOM BOMBS IN MOTION

Twister Time

Nothing frightens like a twister. Hurricanes are larger and cause more damage, but they're not in your face like tornadoes. Meteorologists give names to hurricanes, while twisters are numbered 1–5. In Canada, most high-number twisters occur in southern Ontario, Alberta, Saskatchewan, Manitoba and southern Québec, places with extreme weather variables—our tornado belts.

Saskatchewan and Manitoba's wide-open spaces and proximity to both arctic and maritime air masses moving up from the U.S. make for interesting weather. If storm chasing is your thing, these two provinces are your places—every year sees about a dozen big tornadoes form, but population is sparse, and dozens more go unreported. In 2007, a mostly stationary, now famous F5 made a spectacular but uneventful appearance. Our official biggie, but not our worst by a long shot, as the Big Kahuna of Canadian twisters occurred back in 1912, an F4 they called the Regina Cyclone.

On June 30, 1912, the residents of Regina had suffered through a day that saw temperatures top 40°C. Relief came just before 5:00 PM—the mercury dropped and a cool breeze blew through the streets. What joy, but then from the south came a rattle of thunder and the sky turned black as ink. That was okay; Regina needed rain as every lawn and garden had been parched for weeks.

But what they didn't need made its appearance at 5:00 PM, a tornado of humongous proportions with winds exceeding 350 kilometres per hour. People actually flocked to watch the

400-metre wide monster and then wished they hadn't, because that twister could move fast. For 20 minutes it ravaged the city, destroying homes, the Methodist church, the library and half the business district. It flattened the CPR round-house and threw boxcars into the air like toys. The tornado then turned on the warehouses, exploding them like bombs and turning the area into a war zone.

When it finally ran off onto the prairie and dissipated, it left 28 residents dead, hundreds injured and more than 2000 homeless. Five hundred buildings were destroyed, and the damage totalled $4 million ($1 billion, 2009). A century later, that event still holds the Canadian record for the highest number of deaths attributed to a tornado.

Southern Ontario sees about one-third of all Canadian tornadoes, mostly because of close proximity to the Great Lakes and the Ohio River Valley. During the spring months, warm soggy air from the Gulf of Mexico speeding north through the Ohio Valley will often collide with northeast winds from central Mexico, and if these should encounter cold southeast winds blowing from the Rockies or Arctic, the result can be a dramatic wind shear.

Wind shear is a meteorological term used to describe winds that blow in different directions at different altitudes. When that northerly moving air from the Gulf of Mexico encounters arctic cold, it rises and gets pushed by wind shear into a horizontal rotation. If strong wind shear pushes one way at the bottom and another pushes the opposite way at the top, a horizontally spinning snake-like tube is created.

Ground heat, or heat rising from Great Lakes water will gravi-tate towards the low pressure created from the spinning tube and will pull it down onto the earth where it sucks warm, moist air high into the atmosphere. On the way up, the moist air condenses into water droplets and a thunderhead is created.

However, that air can rise even farther, sometimes to 18 kilometres, where those water droplets freeze into ice crystals. These high, powerful storm clouds called super cells will bombard the earth with hail, lightning, and may spawn multiple funnel clouds.

Tornadoes are horrors, like atom bombs in motion, and while we don't have as many as the U.S., where tracking them has become something of a sport, we do get them on a regular basis, and some have been killers.

Invisible Tornadoes

A tornado can be any colour depending on density, topography and lifespan. An F2 churning up a potato field in rural Prince Edward Island will suck up red soil and look that colour until it gathers debris and darkens to the colour of blood. Yikes!

Worse is a twister touching down in a dry environment. You hear the roar, but it's hard to see until spinning debris accumulates at the funnel base. If there is no debris to collect, you're in trouble.

Everyone has seen a dust devil; if not for the dust it would be almost invisible, so imagine it's big brother touching down on an ice-covered lake or field. Water vapour colours most newly spawned tornadoes white, like clouds. But after a few minutes of sucking up soil, bits of houses, barns, puddles and ponds, the colour darkens and can be black as night.

Worse yet, are tornadoes that come in the night—the F5 that touched down in Elie, Manitoba, in June 2008 spent half its life in darkness. If the reader is Internet connected, go online and see that monster. It's a perfect tornado that lucky for residents remained mostly stationary (travelled 5.5 kilometres) and did minimal damage.

Twisters can move fast, their average speed over the ground is 30 to 50 kilometres per hour, but a few have been clocked at 100 kilometres.

The old adage that what you can't see won't hurt you does not apply to nighttime twisters. During the day, people work or attend school in structures built from concrete and steel, but single family or mobile homes offer little protection from twisters. Awakened by a tornado ripping into your home is the ultimate nightmare.

The most dangerous window of time for a tornado, according to research findings, is the period from midnight to sunrise. Tornadoes during this period are 2.5 times more likely to kill. (Over 60 percent of U.S. tornado fatalities in mobile homes take place at night.)

Tornado Outbreaks

On April 3 and 4, 1974, a single weather system spawned 148 tornadoes and devastated portions of 13 American states and one Canadian province (Ontario). The multiple twisters killed over 300 people, injured almost 5000 and caused damages in excess of a half billion dollars.

A single F3 from this system touched down near Windsor, Ontario, and killed nine, injured 30 and accounted for $2 million in damages to homes and farms.

Tornado outbreaks occur when a large number (six or more) of tornadoes form in groups or individual storms within a 24- to 48-hour period over a specific area and spawn from the same

Hey, Martha! We finally get a break.

general weather system. In the U.S., outbreaks occur every few years but are rarely seen in Canada.

Not really, because on August 7, 1979, a major tornado outbreak struck southwestern Ontario near Woodstock. That outbreak featured two F4 storms that ripped through Woodstock and one F3 storm that smashed into nearby Stratford, killing one and injuring 142.

Multiple tornadoes are terrifying. You can see videos of multiple twisters on YouTube, some of which are from outbreaks, but most are doublets from a single super cell.

CANADA'S KILLER TORNADOES

(courtesy of Environment Canada)

Galt, Ontario—August 7, 1844—one dead, several injured

A minor twister knocked over trees, smashed buildings, and caused one fatality, a woman—Canada's first recorded tornado fatality.

Bouctouche, New Brunswick—August 6, 1879—five dead, 10 injured

A twister thought to be an F3 ripped into Bouctouche, a small town near Moncton, New Brunswick, where it smashed trees, destroyed farms, outbuildings, bridges, a mill, a church and sections of a convent. The tornado caused horrendous property damage and was last seen heading out to sea as a waterspout.

Valleyfield, Québec—August 16, 1888—nine dead, 14 injured

Not much is known about this twister, except that it touched down in Ontario, crossed into Québec at St-Zotique and headed straight for Valleyfield, where it smashed and blew up buildings.

St-Rose, Québec—June 14, 1892—six dead, 26 injured

No information is available due to lack of record keeping. St-Rose is located north of Montréal.

Regina, Saskatchewan—June 30, 1912—28 dead, hundreds injured

Called the Regina Cyclone, it was Canada's most damaging tornadic event. Now rated an F4, this monster, initially a doublet, ripped a swath of destruction through Regina, destroying or severely damaging 500 buildings and laying waste the city's infrastructure. An interesting aside was the presence during the disaster of British actor William Henry Pratt, who volunteered as a rescue worker. Pratt later moved to Hollywood, changed his name to Boris Karloff and made his mark playing the monster in the film *Frankenstein.*

Windsor, Ontario—June 17, 1946—17 dead, hundreds injured

A monster F4 barrelled across the Detroit River, flattened 150 barns and farm buildings and struck the city of Windsor, where it demolished or badly damaged 400 homes. The third worst tornado in Canadian history, and we have an eyewitness account from Windsor resident W.H. Coyle, as related to a reporter from *The Windsor Star*:

> It seemed to have electricity in the center of it. It wasn't black, the way some people have described it. It was gray, the shape of a cone, with the tip toward the earth.
>
> It seemed to bounce along and every time the tip of the cone touched the earth there was a trail of smoke. It just

seemed to pick or suck a house up and grind it to bits, dropping pieces of wood and debris all over the country.

They found 17 bodies, but many people were unaccounted for, and the death toll was probably much higher as the twister took away entire families. Total disaster, but in the end, there emerged a few warm and fuzzy happenings. People came from all over to help, boy scouts mobilized to search for survivors, and the good folks in Detroit sent boxes of flashlights and lamps to be used by local hospitals. Then there was the newspaper incident—power had gone out over most of the city, and the local newspaper, *The Windsor Star,* was unable to publish an account of the storm. The paper hit the streets regardless, having been printed and trucked over by *The Detroit News.* (Note: There are some marvellous photographs of this tornado posted online.)

Sudbury, Ontario—August 20, 1970—six dead, 200 injured

Tornadoes are foreign to the north, and residents of Sudbury were in no way prepared for a monster F3 at their gates. The twister ravaged the city and completely mangled the Inco plant, causing millions of dollars in damages. A strange occurrence that far north, and it got even stranger when an hour later another twister, probably from the same storm cell, chewed up the town of Field some 50 kilometres east of Sudbury.

Windsor, Ontario—April 3, 1974—nine dead, 30 injured

Residents of Windsor talked about the 1946 tornado as if it was a one-time affair and never expecting a redux. However, that is exactly what happened. On April 3, 1974 a historical outbreak of twisters occurred in the U.S.—148 tornadoes touched down in 13 U.S. states over a 16-hour period, killing

330 folks, injuring 5000 and causing a billion dollars in damage. One of those beasts, an F3, bolted across the Detroit River just a half mile from where the '46 tornado made a crossing and became Canada's sixth deadliest twister. It smashed trees, crushed homes, and killed nine people at a curling rink.

Woodstock, Ontario—August 7, 1979—one dead, 142 injured

Residents of Woodstock expected the usual late afternoon breeze, but on August 7, there was only heat waves rising off streets and the incessant chirr of cicadas. Around 6:30 PM, the cicadas stopped chirring, and folks out walking their dogs heard a freight train coming down the tracks. Only the trains no longer passed through Woodstock, and the tracks had been gone for years. What was making the noise? The dogs knew and ran off leaving their masters to ponder. They didn't ponder long and were soon running after their pets. Three monster tornadoes had touched down northeast of Woodstock, and two of the biggest, both F4s, headed straight for town like they had a map, and left hundreds homeless. Not only Woodstock was chewed up, but the entire area also took a thrashing as the twisters cut a swath of destruction over 129 kilometres in what became known as the Woodstock Tornado. More than 600 homes and buildings from Stratford, Ontario, through to Woodstock and Jarvis were destroyed or seriously damaged by twisters packing winds up to 400 kilometres per hour. The communities of Oxford Centre and Vanessa were wiped off the map, and damage was estimated at $100 million. But amazingly, only one person died, the driver of a car blown off the road.

"I watched one of the trees bend way over and then it was gone," said Paul Zilke. "All of a sudden I saw this blue-greenish wall moving steadily up the driveway and I just yelled, 'Tornado. Tornado.'"

In the house were Paul Zilke's father, mother, three brothers and a cousin. All but the father and his youngest brother Andrew (18 months) made it to the basement.

"I guess dad figured he couldn't make it to the basement so he just laid Andrew on the couch and laid over top to protect him....I'll never forget the noise. There were things hitting the house, slamming against the plaster walls and then parts of the house started snapping off, " Paul said.

From behind a tree, Paul watched the tornado smash his family's home into kindling and head off across a field. "I went into the living room and there was dad in a little cubby hole holding Andrew underneath all this debris." The elder Zilke's pelvis had been crushed under the collapsed roof, but young Andrew was fine. While the father stayed motionless, waiting for help to arrive, the rest of the family stumbled out of the ruins.

"We were kind of dazed and confused," Zilke recalls. "There were wires on the ground and I remember standing there and just taking in all of the destruction. The corn field was flat." (Paul Zilke's Woodstock tornado story courtesy of *The London Free Press*.)

After the Woodstock Tornado—The Warm and Fuzzy

Before the tornado struck, Woodstock had been suffering through tough economic times from several factory closings—the tornadoes destroyed or seriously damaged nine more companies, putting almost the entire labour force out of work. With no jobs and 1000 families homeless, despair and loneliness loomed over the small town of Woodstock.

But within hours of the disaster, Woodstock and surrounding areas discovered they were not going to be left alone in their misery. The relief effort was immediate, but the emergency shelters set up by the Red Cross and YWCA went unused as friends and family opened their doors to the victims. Then a kind of miracle happened. Help arrived from everywhere: volunteers poured into the community, ambulances arrived from nearby towns, local businesses set up drop-off centres for donations ranging from cash to clothes and food, and the Ontario government pledged $1 in relief for every dollar donated.

A local radio station held a 10-hour radio appeal that raised $450,000, and other municipalities sent tens of thousands of dollars. Makes a reader all warm and fuzzy, but it gets even better. The day after the blow, area Mennonites began arriving in town by the hundreds. They had come to help clean up, and they stayed to help folks rebuild.

Makes you proud to be a Canadian, eh?

Barrie, Ontario—May 31, 1985—eight dead, 155 injured

The area around Barrie and Lake Simcoe is no stranger to tornadoes; every year the media reports a few small ones touching down and tearing up hay, tipping cows and dissipating. Very few residents of Barrie had seen one of these, let alone a big twister.

All that changed on May 31, a few minutes before 5:00 PM, when a monster F4 touched down a few kilometres southwest of town. The beast was 600 metres wide and black as sin; they know the width because as it headed for Barrie, the twister had smashed through a pine forest cutting a swath that wide. After the forest, the twister burst into town and took out an entire block of older frame houses causing three fatalities. Next came an industrial park, where it destroyed or badly damaged 16 factories and caused one fatality. Luckily, the power had failed some hours earlier, and most of the workers had left the buildings.

The Barrie racetrack was next—it wrecked barns, tossed around trucks and trailers and caused horses to stampede for their lives. The twister then crossed a major highway, heaving cars and trucks into nearby fields.

A subdivision came next, and the swath of destruction had shrunk to 300 metres. A few minutes later, at another industrial park, it smashed 11 factories before shrinking to 100 metres. The monster was progressively weakening, but it had enough power left to pulverize another subdivision, causing another four fatalities. Finally, after smashing up a local marina, the almost spent tornado turned and headed out into Lake Simcoe where is dissipated. The marina would later report that it took along 35 boats with their concrete mooring anchors.

Edmonton, Alberta—July 31, 1987—27 dead, 253 injured

July 31, 1987, started out as just another hot summer day in Edmonton, but a few minutes before noon, the skies darkened, the temperature dropped and it began to rain. Torrential rain, and it flooded rivers and pelted the city with hailstones.

Bad got worse at about 3:00 PM—a black funnel cloud touched down, making a noise like a dozen freight trains. Not pausing for a second, the monster swept northward through downtown Edmonton, ripping the city from stem to stern. Canada's second-worst tornado, and it killed 27 people, injured hundreds and left 1000 residents without homes. Winds topped 416 kilometres per hour—and now rated an F4 tornado, that monster cut a swath of death and destruction 40 kilometres long and as much as one kilometre wide.

At a place called Evergreen Mobile Home Park, the tornado destroyed 200 of 600 trailers and killed 15 people.

Rosa-St. Malo, Manitoba—1997—three dead, many injured

Rosa-St. Malo is a northern Manitoba resort town of 1000 people, with no newspaper and a narrow mindset. F4 tornadoes are scary phenomena, especially to the many Rosa-St. Malo trailer camp operators who think if your words can't promote the place, don't open your mouth. They didn't, because other than the grim fact that it killed three people, there's not a word anywhere about the town's tornado experience. And they still don't, because my three questioning phone calls to people in Rosa-St. Malo who should know, all received "no comment" answers.

Pine Lake, Alberta—July 14, 2000—12 dead, 140 injured

Pine Lake is located 150 kilometres northeast of Calgary in a popular recreational area, particularly on this midsummer weekend.

Shortly after noon on the 14th, thunderstorms formed over the foothills of the Rocky Mountains in western Alberta then moved northeastwardly across the plains. A narrow band of low-level moist air lay to the south of the storm's trajectory, giving enough instability to the air for the thunderstorms to form into a super cell. Environment Canada issued a severe thunderstorm watch at 5:37 PM MDT for the region surrounding Red Deer, which included Pine Lake, and about 40 minutes later upgraded the watch to a warning.

At approximately 7:00 PM, a tornado formed within the cell and touched down five kilometres west of the Green Acres Campground at Pine Lake. Accompanied by baseball–size hail, that twister made a beeline for the camp and surprised over 700 campers gathered for their evening meal. The F3 tornado ripped through tents and recreational vehicles cutting a swath of destruction 800 to 1500 metres wide. It tossed trailers, boats and other vehicles into the lake along with several individuals, who somehow survived and swam ashore.

In the end, emergency workers set the official casualty list at nine dead and 132 severely injured. Hundreds of others received minor injuries and were treated onsite. Those with severe injuries were evacuated to hospitals in nearby Red Deer as well as Calgary and Edmonton. Three of those died in intensive care units from their injuries, raising the final death toll to 12.

Gull Lake, Manitoba—August 6, 2006—one dead, 12 injured

Twisters love to beat up on trailer parks. An improbable statement, but it sure seems that way. The Gull Lake tornado spawned from a thunderstorm containing three funnel clouds, none with enough power to reach ground. But when the storm passed over Gull Lake, 80 kilometres northeast of Winnipeg, it seemed unable to resist a trailer park nestled beside the lake. Three funnels suddenly joined into a tornado and wrecked every trailer in the park, causing one fatality.

Don't think that's the lot. Canada is second in the world (behind the U.S.) for numbers of tornadoes. We have our own tornado alleys, and many people are killed by undocumented tornadoes. If a twister wipes out a trailer park and no one survives to authenticate a tornado, local authorities chalk it up as a violent thunderstorm.

Elie, Manitoba—June 22, 2007

Second in the world for number of tornadoes, and we only documented our first F5 twister on June 22, 2007. F5 is at the top of the Fujita tornado damage scale with winds that can exceed 500 kilometres per hour. That monster terrorized the residents of Elie, Manitoba, for 35 minutes but remained mostly stationary. It wrecked some of their stuff and left, and the good people of Elie had a story to tell their grandchildren.

Note: Contrary to popular belief, trailer parks do not attract tornadoes.

TORNADO SAFETY

Emergency Procedures

Here is a list of what to do if confronted by a tornado (from Environment Canada):

- Take shelter immediately, if available, preferably in the lower level of a sturdy building.

- Stay away from windows, doors and exterior walls. Flying glass is extremely dangerous.

- Don't waste time opening windows to keep pressure from building up in the house. It's unlikely to help anyway.

- If you're outdoors with no shelter available, lie flat in a ditch, ravine or other low-lying area, and shield your head with your arms.

- Don't get caught in a vehicle or mobile home, which the tornado can lift. Take shelter elsewhere or, if none is available, even a ditch offers better protection. Choose a location where your vehicle won't be hurled or rolled on top of you. More than half of tornado deaths occur in mobile homes. If you live in a mobile home, it is wise to identify a nearby sturdy shelter well in advance, and go to that shelter when a severe storm is approaching.

- Beware of flying debris. Even small objects such as sticks and straw can become lethal missiles.

- In heavy rain, be on the lookout for flash floods.

- When swimming or boating, always head to shore at the first sight of a storm.

- Remember that damaged and weakened structures, fallen debris, downed electrical wires and gas leaks are potential dangers after a storm has passed.

Best Shelter

- In a house, go to the basement and take shelter under a stairway or a sturdy worktable in the centre of the house.

- In a house with no basement, the safest spot is the ground floor in the centre of the house. Small rooms tend to be more structurally sound, so seek shelter in a hallway, small room, closet or bathroom (the plumbing may provide some structural stability). Lying in the bathtub with a mattress on top of you may also provide good protection.

- If you're in a vehicle or mobile home, get outside and find other shelter. North American officials still debate whether seeking shelter in a vehicle during a tornado is safe. Some advise that if the tornado is weak, a vehicle can offer protection against flying debris and rollovers if the occupants fasten seat belts and keep their heads down. However, there is no way of knowing how strong or violent a tornado is without the proper tools, so the safest strategy is to get out of the vehicle. As a last resort, lie in a ditch or culvert, but be aware of flooding.

- Avoid wide-span buildings, such as barns, auditoriums, shopping centres and supermarkets with large roofs. Go to a nearby sturdy shelter, preferably, or to the lower floor, an inside room, restroom or hallway, or get underneath a sturdy piece of furniture. At school, seek shelter in a small windowless room such as a washroom, instead of a gymnasium. Avoid areas near high walls or large chimneys that may collapse. In shopping centres, stay out of aisles and away from exterior walls and windows. Do not go to your parked vehicle.

- In high-rise buildings, move to lower levels, small interior rooms or stairwells. Stay away from elevators and windows.

Note: A little something the good folks at Environment Canada left out…

Never try to outrun a tornado in your vehicle; instead, find a road at right angles to the twister and stomp hard on the gas pedal. Tornadoes can move quick and straight, while Martha must navigate curves and bends in the road. If you're caught on foot in an open area with no culverts or ditches, do not panic. First, ascertain the direction of the tornado, then panic, and run like the devil's on your heels at a right angle from the horror. Oh, and never, never look over your shoulder at a twister…it will eat you.

Scary Phenomena

Violent thunderstorms have terrorized children and put the fear of God into adults for millenniums. The stuff of nightmares, but other weather phenomena go bump in the night and can be even more nightmarish.

THESE WILL BOUNCE YOUR REALITY CHECK

Downbursts

What goes up, must come down is a Newtonian axiom for everything, including air. It rises and falls, and most times does so gently. But occasionally, an up-building thunderstorm will vacuum dry air into its rising column and shoot it skyward. Rising quickly, the dry air absorbs vapour from the saturated cloud through evaporation, much like a refrigerator. By the time the dry air in the column reaches the top of the giant storm cloud, it's saturated with vapour and icy cold. Now free of the updraft, this cold, dense air falls like a rock.

Some old-timers call this falling air a plow wind, because its going straight down at speeds that can top 200 kilometres per hour and plows into the ground, smashing down like a giant hammer and moving outwards with a terrifying noise. It sounds like a tornado, and many victims of downdraft events are convinced a twister has mauled them. These things can be any size and duration depending on the storm. If the storm cell is large and spread out, the downdraft it creates, called a macro, is usually accompanied by high winds, rain, and sometimes, hail. If the storm is a super cell, a single entity, you can expect a smaller-diameter, micro-downdraft, with tornado-strength winds that cause severe damage to trees and buildings. Downdrafts are deadly to small boats, landing aircraft, and people walking dogs in rainstorms.

Multiple downbursts may sometimes occur in elongated storm cells that cover many kilometres and have been known to smash down entire forests. These are called derecho storms, and in

July 1995, a derecho ravaged upstate New York, knocking down over one million acres of trees.

Sometimes downburst air can become compressed on the way down releasing heat; meteorologists call this a heat burst and temperature rises in excess of 10°C have been recorded.

Drought

Contrary to common belief that the southern prairies are semi-arid, the average climate of the region is actually humid to subhumid. The subhumid zone is almost entirely contained within the Palliser Triangle, delineated by Captain John Palliser in the 1850s as the driest region of the prairies. During periods of drought, much of the southern prairies are dominated by semi-arid conditions. Although the average climate of the southern prairies is subhumid, droughts create extreme conditions that are distinctly semi-arid. Confused? Just think of the prairie climate as being mostly pleasant, but capable of supporting cacti that grow in some areas. These recurrent extremes necessitate that the flora, fauna and people of the region be well adapted to semi-arid conditions.

Drought affects countries around the world, and for Canada's prairie provinces, it's the main climatic concern. Wheat is a grass, and although the plants are heat tolerant with deep roots, they do not fare well in prolonged periods of near zero precipitation. The crop suffers, as do the grassy pasturelands for livestock. Cattle and wheat are the lifeblood of the prairies, and droughts can drastically reduce production. A drought in 2002 resulted in one of the worst harvests in Canadian history. In 1987–88, drought-related losses in western Canada exceeded $2 billion, and many farmers and ranchers were forced out of business. In the Dirty Thirties, the infamous dustbowl drought nearly wiped out the entire agricultural industry.

Droughts can also affect shipping on the Great Lakes. During the drought of 2002, diminished water levels forced cargo ships to reduce loads by 100 metric tons for every 2.5 centimetres the lake levels fell.

Wildfires are more common during droughts and cost millions of dollars to fight. Recreation and tourist industries suffer: fishing streams dry up, ski resorts have little snow, campfires are *verboten* in forests, and hungry wildlife may turn aggressive.

Although droughts are weather related and not climatic, they may become more climatic because of our planet's warming trend, and our drought-vulnerable prairie provinces may require a switch to crops requiring less water. Fallow crops, such as beans, mustard and canola, may become permanent, while "king wheat" fades in importance. On the other hand, our planet's recent warming trend may push warm cells traversing the U.S. Midwest farther north, treating our prairies to increased precipitation with more bountiful wheat production. It's a flip of the coin; nobody knows what will happen, and we'll just have to cross our fingers and hope we don't see a return of the Dirty Thirties.

Dust Storms

Dust storms are a frequent occurrence during droughts and are most frequent on the U.S. Great Plains states and Canada's prairie provinces. Called "dusters" by locals, these storms are caused by strong winds picking up small grains of earth and raising them into the atmosphere as a large cloud wall that may have a front many kilometres wide and a height in excess of 1000 metres.

Dusters may at times be preceded by dust devils, mini tornadoes either attached or separate from the wall, and these should be avoided, as they can be powerful and very dangerous. Dust storms from the African continent frequently cross the Atlantic and deposit sand on both the South and North

American continents. Inversely, dust from storms originating in the Canadian prairies and U.S. plains has been spotted in the middle of the Atlantic, apparently headed for Africa.

Storm Surge

Surge occurs when coastal sea levels rise as a result of high onshore winds that "pile up" water ahead of the storm. It is also common during approaching hurricanes when the sea is pulled upward by extreme low pressure. Storm surge can also occur when a hurricane does not make landfall but moves along the coast. In 1869, in New Brunswick and western Nova Scotia, a hurricane called the Saxby Gale pushed tides two metres above normal, flooding lowland areas and causing many fatalities. A storm surge often causes more damage than a hurricane. Twenty-four hours before the 2007 onslaught of Hurricane Gustav on the U.S. Gulf Coast, a four-metre-high wall of water surprised many residents of New Orleans before they could evacuate the city, causing many fatalities.

Surprise surges can kill, and with 243,000 kilometres of coastline, Canada has been surprised more than a few times. On October 4, 1869, that infamous Saxby Gale piled seawater into New Brunswick's Bay of Fundy at high tide, creating a monster tidal bore that sank ships, overran dikes, flooded low-lying areas and killed more than 90 people. This combination of high tide and storm surge will occur there again eventually, and since sea levels have risen every year since 1869, the results could be more catastrophic. This could have happened on September 29, 2003, when that hurricane called Juan barrelled into Nova Scotia during low tide, killing eight people and causing over $100 million in damages. If Juan had made landfall during high tide, the damage and loss of life would have been unbelievable.

Luck has a great bearing on weather disasters; that 1869 Saxby Gale surge killed New Brunswick's Fundy Bay farmers in the act of saving their livestock from the hurricane. It also killed fishermen trying to ride out the storm. But except for the high waves and heavy rain, it hardly touched Nova Scotia. Those folks were lucky; the farmers and fishermen were not.

Note: The Saxby Gale is named after Stephen Saxby, an instructor in the Royal Navy who, 10 months before the event, wrote a letter to the *London Standard* newspaper warning that on October 5, 1869, the tides in the North Atlantic would be extremely high during hurricane season, and a devastating storm would ensue. Nobody paid any attention to Saxby until after the fact. They apologized, by giving his name to the storm; a consolation prize probably not much appreciated by the victims' families.

Lake Seiche

A seiche is a non-frightening event and only mentioned because of its relationship with storm surge. Storm surge events are not confined to Canada's coastlines; they can occur in large bodies of fresh water, especially in the Great Lakes, where they are called seiche (pronounced "saysh")—think water sloshing in a bathtub with a low-pressure storm at one end doing the sloshing instead of a kid. All the Great Lakes have a perpetual seiche of a few centimetres that goes mostly unnoticed, while some, like Lake Ontario, have a very pronounced seiche when winds blow from the southwest. Winds from that direction surge water from Rochester, New York, to the Bay of Quinte, a distance of 110 kilometres, and after the winds abate, back and forth goes the water like in a bathtub. This pendulum effect can go on for days and provides one of Ontario's rivers with a tide. Lake seiche causes water to slosh up and down the Napanee River in one hour and six-minute increments you can set your watch by.

Lake Erie is a long, shallow lake prone to wind-driven seiche that can sometimes exceed five metres. In September 1985, a wind-driven seiche overran Long Point and swept 40 cottages into the lake. Luckily, it was off-season, and only property was lost.

Back in 1954, luck ran out for eight shore fishermen from Chicago, Illinois, when a three-meter-high seiche washed them off a breakwater into Lake Michigan. The water just rose up, caught them by surprise and drowned the lot. Weird, but even more weird is that the same thing had happened 20 years earlier in almost the same spot, when a seiche wave suddenly rose up onto a Chicago beach, drowning a dozen bathers.

In 1954, Hurricane Hazel's winds, which decimated Toronto, created a seiche in Lake Ontario that sloshed back and forth longitudinally, flooding both the city's waterfront and large areas of the American south shore. Even when the storm had passed, the seiche kept sloshing for days.

Wind-driven seiche can have a major impact on Great Lakes shorelines, causing erosion and damage to piers and breakwaters. During a November 1972 storm on Lake Erie, northeast winds reached a constant speed in excess of 50 kilometres per hour, and the seiche inflicted millions of dollars of damage to both U.S. and Canadian shorelines.

Mega Tsunami, or Iminami

Going on vacation to the South Seas this winter? Hawaii, perhaps? Or maybe you've set your sights on the Atlantic side; some place like the Canary Islands? Every winter, people flock to these popular tourist destinations unaware that these places are simply piles of volcanic rubble with their tops sticking above water like icebergs. Volcanic islands have a lot in common with icebergs, both are formed by layering, both are unstable, and both are prone to splitting and slumping large chunks into the ogen (sailor slang for "ocean"). Not a problem with icebergs, but if an island drops a large chunk of undersea topography, the results can be catastrophic, and evidence points to this happening on a regular basis. Scientists have discovered debris fields around the bottom of almost every island of volcanic origin. Most do slump, but usually not enough at one time to be dangerous.

The keyword here is "usually," because there have been some mega tsunamis caused by slumping. Earthquakes lowering or raising the seabed cause most, and these can be devastating. Iminamis, or mega tsunamis, are usually the result of catastrophic impact: landslide, volcanic eruption or comets hitting the earth. These waves can wipe entire cultures off the map—as it did the Minoans, when around 1500 BC, a volcanic eruption blew up half the island of Santorini. Pity the Minoans, but the blast created a wave that devastated the entire Mediterranean coastline, and who knows what other cultures were swept away.

Centuries later, on October 9, 1963, a landslide tore into the lake above Italy's Vajont Dam and created a 250-metre-high mega tsunami that roared across the lake, overran the dam and destroyed five villages, killing 2000 inhabitants.

Closer to home, in Alaska on July 9, 1950, an earthquake ripped loose a huge chunk of topography at the end of Lituya Bay, a fiord in Alaska's Glacier National Park, and created a wave so high it inundated the deep fiord's opposite bank, wiping it clean of trees and soil and leaving only bedrock. Hardly a noteworthy event, until you consider that the opposite bank is over 524 metres high, enough height to deploy a parachute. That wave then scoured its way down the fiord and emptied into the sea, but not before encountering a small fishing boat with two occupants.

I am reminded of this event every few years and can never help but wonder what last words those two victims had for each other. What does one say when confronting a wall of water over 500 metres high?

Vacationers should be especially leery of the Canary Islands, as geologists believe this to be the next source of a mega tsunami. During a 1949 volcanic eruption on the biggest of the Canary Islands, Las Palma, an earthquake caused a volcanic ridge covering one-third of the island to fracture, and slip one metre sideways and two metres down. It now hangs like a sword of Damocles awaiting another quake to shake it loose, a fact never mentioned in their travel brochures. Considering that particular topography weighs somewhere in the area of

500 billion tons, the splash will be immense, and scientists predict a wave several hundred metres high.

But staying home may not help, because a wave of that magnitude just might reach around the globe and will probably strike the eastern seaboard of North America with a series of waves 25 to 50 metres high capable of travelling 10 to 20 kilometres inland. Scary stuff, and those millions of folks living on the eastern seaboard having to evacuate quickly is even scarier. Our over-urbanized populations do not evacuate well, mostly because they have nowhere to go. In the old days, people just headed west or to the family farm, but that egress no longer flies.

Canada has its own sword of Damocles. It's called Mt. Breckenridge, and it looms over one of Canada's most famous spa resorts, Harrison Hot Springs in British Columbia.

Mountains are intrinsically high on the danger scale, but Mt. Breckenridge is over-the-top dangerous because of fracturing. Geologists have identified one area that could let go at any time and fall into the very deep Lake Harrison. Experts think the splash would generate a mega tsunami and wipe out all life along the length of the Harrison River, parts of the Fraser River Valley and sections of Washington State.

Sounds ominous, but we'll just have to wait and see what happens, as nobody can do anything about it except shake heads and talk. Meanwhile, as the clock ticks, business is booming at Harrison Hot Springs, and tourists hardly ever ask about the bits of rock in the bathing pool.

Hypercane

These are enormous "things can always be worse" super hurricanes with winds in excess of 800 kilometres per hour that may have occurred in ancient times but have so far spared the modern world a visit. The Massachusetts Institute of Technology (MIT) has computer-modelled hypercanes and theorizes two causes: an ocean-impacting meteor heating water above 49°C, and a large undersea volcanic eruption heating local seas above that same temperature. The good news is that MIT's computer models only have a 24-kilometre-wide vortice. The bad news is the vortice would fire water vapour 40 kilometres into the upper atmosphere and cause massive global weather problems.

Blizzards

Environment Canada officially classifies a blizzard as having these components: snow or blowing snow with winds of 40 kilometres per hour or more, visibility reduced to one kilometre,

a wind chill of –25°C or colder, and lasting four hours or more. A conservative yardstick for a weather phenomenon capable of putting the brakes on all our worldly activities. You have to be able to see to do almost anything, and if you can't, better stop. Which is what our transcontinental railways did in Alberta and Saskatchewan between January 30 and February 8, 1947, when blowing snow buried tracks and some trains under 10-metre-high drifts. Blinding snow continued for 10 days, immobilizing Calgary, Edmonton and all the towns and villages in between. When the blizzard finally quit and people dug themselves out, all they could see were the tops of trees and telephone poles. Some communities remained stranded for months, and it took weeks to get the tracks cleared and the trains running again.

Bad, but on the other hand, without blizzards we may not have enjoyed the expedient luxury of subway systems, for a blizzard created the impetus for that invention. The Great Blizzard of 1888 caused all manner of rail traffic chaos in New York City: trains collided, stalled in mid-journey or were stuck on elevated tracks. This had happened too many times, and the city fathers decided to do something about it—and that something was the world's first subway. Genius always rises, just like cream.

There are two types of blizzards: a regular precipitation blizzard, and ground blizzards, where the precipitation is already present and snow is moved by strong winds. Ground blizzards are divided into three categories: horizontal advection, where the wind blows across the surface; vertical advection, where the wind lofts snow upwards creating large drifting waves; and thermal-mechanical, where both wind and updrafts create massive rolling waves called snow billows. Billowing occurs mostly in arctic areas and is extremely dangerous, as it makes vision almost impossible and breathing difficult. Ground blizzards occur mostly on vast open areas without trees to catch snow.

Open areas are more susceptible, such as Lake Erie and Ontario, where in the weeks before the new year of 1977, a shifting arctic air mass caused migrating warm air from the U.S. Midwest to dump massive amounts of snow onto the frozen lakes where, because of the cold, it stayed dry, fluffy and ready to shuffle off to Buffalo. On January 27, 1977, a cascading arctic cold front slammed onto frozen Lake Erie and all that dry snow shuffled off to become the infamous Blizzard of '77, a storm that caused major problems for southern Ontario's Niagara region...and Buffalo, New York.

The following passage is from Erno Rossi's classic book on that blizzard, *White Death: The Blizzard of '77,* and it illustrates the fury of the blizzard as it hit that day. It's the account of a school-teacher who had to walk from a friend's house to his home on the Lake Erie shoreline in Port Colborne, Ontario, normally a pleasant three-mile walk.

> I started walking and…I had no idea where I was. It hurt my eyes to stare at things. I felt crunching under my feet and I thought, my God, this is a little different. I bent over and felt with my hands.… I realized I wasn't on the road. I was on Lake Erie! Ice under my feet! I started running. I was terrified.… Then I spotted a dark shadow and I ran for it. It happened to be a tree, thank God! … I was on my hands and knees half of the time crawling.… Finally, I spotted my place. Oh God,…I was so excited.

Attila Nagy, another teacher from Port Colborne said this about the blizzard:

> The blizzard came on so suddenly everything stopped: motorists abandoned their vehicles, the snow plows gave up, and school officials kept hundreds of students at school. People waited in cars or businesses to ride out the storm hoping to continue back home later that day. But the storm didn't subside. The severe blizzard continued through the night into the next day.

That blizzard hit the Niagara area hard, but it was Buffalo, New York, that bore the brunt. In his book *The Blizzard,* author Robert Bahr describes conditions in Buffalo as the arctic front came through late that Friday morning from the perspective of businessman Larry Mark during a meeting on the 16th floor of a downtown building.

> The room grew silent. Everyone turned to the windows. They heard a roar an instant before the wind struck

the building. Larry felt the floor shudder and heard the plate glass creak. Sixteen floors below, shoppers and businessmen staggered into the wind. Some clung to streetlight poles and traffic signs; others ducked for shelter. A man's hat soared high above traffic....The instant the white wave struck the window, Larry wondered if the world might be ending.

The time was 11:10 AM.

Buffalo and its surrounding suburbs were snowed in for weeks. A state of emergency was put into effect by the U.S. government, which included a complete driving ban for over one week in Buffalo. They called in the National Guard to aid in snow removal as some drifts were up to the rooftops.

Hey, Martha! Nobody was ready for that blizzard. We should put together an emergency kit for the car.

Blizzard Survival Kit

(courtesy of Environment Canada)

- Antifreeze
- Axe or hatchet
- Blanket
- Booster cables
- Candle and matches
- Compass
- Emergency food pack
- Extra clothing and footwear
- Fire extinguisher
- First-aid kit
- Flashlight and new batteries
- Ice scraper and brush
- Salt
- Sand
- Shovel
- Tow Chain
- Warning light or road flares

Pine Smog

Canada is pine tree heaven; we have billions, and every one is pumping volatile chemicals into the air we breathe. Waxes, nitrous oxides and terpenes all smell nice and healthy, but when airborne and in contact with sunshine and ozone pollution, they form aerosols (microscopic solids suspended in air) similar to industrial and automobile emissions. Water molecules are attracted to aerosols and can form snowflakes or rain drops. Nice, because rain and snow cleanse the air and make it well again. Not nice are companies that clear huge tracts of forest for large-scale lumbering and farming operations...cough, cough.

Large-scale planting of pine trees to act as "carbon sinks" has been promoted by scientists all over the world, the theory being that fast-growing trees absorb and retain carbon dioxide from the air. Carbon dioxide is widely cited as one of the major contributors to global warming. Planting pines was considered a good thing, until researchers in Australia discovered pine trees were producing nitrogen oxide. Nitrogen oxides are smog precursors: they combine with other pollutants to form ground-level ozone, a major component of smog.

The researchers found that while the amounts produced were insignificant on a local scale, their findings suggest that global nitrogen oxide issuing from boreal coniferous forests may be comparable to those produced by worldwide industrial and traffic sources.

You will not hear a word about pine smog from the green-for-bucks media crowd since it rubs their spiel the wrong way, but it's out there, and it's coming out of our forests like having two vehicles in every garage in the country.

Lightning

When I'm on a golf course and it starts to rain and lightning, I hold up my one iron, 'cause I know even God can't hit a one iron.

–Lee Trevino

STRUCK FROM ABOVE

Pyrotechnic Phenomena

The storm has passed and only a rumble on the horizon reminds of the downpour. You climb into the golf cart, or head back to the garden, but suddenly recall an old adage, *if you can hear the thunder, the lightning can find you,* and you wisely delay resuming your activity. Better to be safe than sorry, and your wisdom is rewarded when lightning explodes a nearby tree while you're talking to your sister Martha on the telephone.

Yes, the adage is true; if you hear it, it can get you, and it gets a few Canadians every year. Lightning kills on average 10 Canadians every year, but that's not the whole story, because it also wounds and maims hundreds, and most strikes go unreported. Lightning can cripple, blind and mentally incapacitate its victims. But you were wise, and the lightning bolt only struck a tree. Then again, maybe not so wise, because had that bolt struck the telephone pole next to that tree, your sister might have been talking on a dead line. There are not a whole lot of places where lightning can't find you. It can enter your home through telephone lines and plumbing, but as long as you're not talking to Martha on the phone, or soaking in the bath or hot tub, it won't harm you.

Warning: do not take a bath or shower during thunderstorms, do not talk to Martha on the telephone, and do not stand near windows to watch the pyrotechnics. If you live in a newer house with PCV pipes, get a lightning arrester installed, because that type of piping will not ground a strike.

Lightning also can be a supreme hazard to boaters, because the vessel is usually the highest object on the water. Fibreglass and wood sailboats are especially vulnerable—their masts are up there like plugs on an electrical cord, and their construction materials are unsuited for grounding electrical charges unless the hull is wet from rainfall. Lightning will cause catastrophic damage to wood or fibreglass boats and their occupants, the worst on record being the 43-metre wooden drill scow *John B. King.* That scow, with a crew of 41, was the largest drilling platform in Canada, and in June 1930 was under contract to deepen channels in the upper reaches of the St. Lawrence River known as the Thousand Islands.

Deepening channels meant blasting with dynamite, and at a place called the Brockville narrows, near Brockville, Ontario, the *John B.* lay at anchor setting underwater charges when a summer thunderstorm developed. The captain immediately ordered up anchor, and had almost cleared the area when lightning struck, igniting the submerged charges and the ship's stores of dynamite. The explosion disintegrated the entire vessel, sending pieces hundreds of metres into the air and killing all but 11 of the 41 crewmen.

A nasty business that could happen to you if caught on the water by a thunderstorm. Your boat may not explode like the *John B.,* but dead is dead—so stay away from thunderstorms while boating.

An automobile or truck makes for excellent protection during a thunderstorm, but not for the reason most people think… the rubber tires. It's the skin effect, which occurs when lightning strikes a metal car or truck body and travels over its surface—it's the roof and sides that save you from terminal zap. The same is not true for riding lawnmowers, golf carts or bikes. Those vehicles are death traps; if a thunderstorm catches you riding one of those, stop and bail out quickly. Vehicles with fibreglass bodies should be pulled to the side of the road, with the occupants sitting with hands folded until the storm passes. This is a good idea in any vehicle: keep your hands folded, do not touch any metal objects,

and keep the windows closed. Lightning striking an automobile will usually pick the radio antenna or a windshield wiper to exit. Either will temporarily blind the driver with a bright flash, so best to pull over until the storm passes. Chances are good you will never be struck by lightning; according to Environment Canada, you have a one in 4000 chance of being zapped in your lifetime. Not bad odds, but some Canadians, the author included, have defied those odds and been struck numerous times, so why gamble; it's always better to be safe than crispy.

Bolt from the Blue

Except for dark clouds on the horizon and a distant rumble of thunder, the storm has passed. Golfers take to their carts, carpenters return to hammering, gardeners dig, and dog walkers hit the sidewalks. A scenario repeated over and over that sometimes leads to tragedy. Meteorologists call it "clear air lightning," because it seemingly strikes without source.

After a storm, blue sky and sunshine return, and suddenly, without any crack of thunder, a golf cart or tree explodes. It's a rare phenomena and little understood, but every year it claims a few more victims. Contrary to the 95 percent of lightning strikes that are negatively charged, bolts from the blue are positive energy originating in the anvils of high-altitude altocumulus clouds. Because of this high origin, targets as far away as 20 or more kilometres can be struck at any time and in clear weather. If that passed-over storm cloud on the horizon has a top shaped like a blacksmith's anvil, you should put off going outside for a few more minutes.

Dry-Air Lightning

This phenomenon is related to clear-air lightning but is less rare and kills more people. The storm has passed, the sky is still overcast, but the rain has stopped and a pleasant dry wind has people resuming their normal activities. But then, seemingly from out of nowhere, ZAP! But how can that be? No rain, and the air is dry. Doesn't air have to be wet to conduct electricity? Yes, normally, but on occasion, tall objects will remain electrically charged after a storm has passed and can sometimes be observed sparking out a blue flame called St. Elmo's Fire, named after the patron saint of sailors, St. Erasmus of Formiae.

A word of warning: if you see this phenomenon, hit the dirt and make like a pancake. Unable to release its negative charge to the atmosphere, that tall sparking object is searching out a suitable ground, which could be you walking the dog. Tall trees, church steeples, telephone poles—it can come from anywhere, so be aware.

Be lightning wise, and to help you out, here are a few tips from Environment Canada.

Learn the 30-30 rule: Take appropriate shelter when you can count 30 seconds or less between the lightning flash and thunder. Remain sheltered for 30 minutes after the last thunderclap.

Outdoor Precautions

- Keep a safe distance from tall objects, such as trees, hilltops and telephone poles.

- Avoid projecting yourself above the surrounding landscape. Seek shelter in low-lying areas such as valleys, ditches and depressions—but be aware of flooding.

- Stay away from water. Do not go boating or swimming if a storm threatens, and land as quickly as possible if on the water. Lightning can strike the water and travel some distance from its point of contact. Don't stand in puddles even if you are wearing rubber boots.

- Stay away from objects that conduct electricity, such as tractors, golf carts, golf clubs, metal fences, motorcycles, lawnmowers and bicycles.

- Avoid being the highest point in an open area. Swinging a golf club or holding an umbrella or fishing rod can make you the tallest object and a target for lightning. Take off shoes with metal cleats. If you're caught in a level field far from shelter and feel your hair stand on end, lightning may be about to hit you. Kneel on the ground immediately, with feet together, place your hands on your knees and bend forward. Do not lie flat. The object here is to make as small a target as possible.

- You are safe inside a vehicle during lightning, but don't park near or under trees or other tall objects that may topple over during a storm. Be aware of downed power lines that may be touching your car. You'll be safe inside the car, but you may receive a shock if you step outside.

- In a forest, seek shelter in a low-lying area under a thick growth of small trees or bushes.

- Keep alert for flash floods, sometimes caused by heavy rainfall, if seeking shelter in a ditch or low-lying area.

- If you are in a group in the open, spread out and keep people several metres apart.

Indoor Precautions

- Before the storm hits, disconnect electrical appliances, including radios and television sets. Do not touch them during the storm.

- Don't go outside unless absolutely necessary.

- Keep away from doors, windows, fireplaces, and anything that will conduct electricity, such as radiators, stoves, sinks and metal pipes. Keep as many walls as possible between you and the outside.

- Don't handle electrical equipment or telephones. Use battery-operated appliances only.

Note: Persons struck by lightning receive an electrical shock but do not hold a charge and can be safely handled. Victims may be suffering from burns or shock and should receive medical attention immediately. If breathing has stopped, mouth-to-mouth resuscitation should be administered. If breathing and pulse are absent, cardiopulmonary resuscitation (CPR) is required. Send for help immediately—if on a golf course look for the course marshal or ranger; he will have a defibrillator and know how to use it.

Lightning is basically a kid shuffling feet on granny's thick carpet while chasing his siblings around. Same spark, just much bigger, the average being around 30,000 amps. But on occasions lightning amperage can rise dramatically to an astounding 300,000 plus amps. These super bolts are six or seven times hotter than the sun and very destructive. If struck by one of these…you're toast. Super bolts have struck baseball fields, killing players; have fried golfers; set barns and houses on fire; burned forests; and knocked down power transmission towers. They like transmission towers, and smashing them costs Canadians $10 million every year. But thankfully, super bolts are rare, and your chances of being fried by a normal bolt are more common, as are your chances of surviving.

Most folks struck by lightning do survive and go about their business as if nothing happened, which explains why official records should not be trusted. Many folks getting the zap never report it. Report to whom? Most strike victims only tell their friends and loved ones, and official reports require proof. The only reporting comes from the police and hospitals, where the proof is still smoking and smelling indisputable.

Super bolts carry a positive rather than a negative charge and come from those flattened tops of altocumulus clouds that meteorologists call the anvil. This is a place of great atmospheric activity caused by warm, moist air rising in the great clouds' updraft and colliding with cold air at the top. How cold? To put this into perspective, a satellite with temp-measuring abilities overflew tropical cyclone Hilda east of Australia in 1990 and measured temps at a top altitude of 18.9 kilometres. The result was a fair dinkum −102.2°C, a temperature difference of 97.2°C between top and bottom.

At such low temps, water droplets freeze hard as titanium and release energy that's off the scale. Positive lightning, or super bolts, can strike the earth far from any storm activity, and for this reason are called out-of-the-blue strikes. The storm is over, lots of sunshine, life is good again—and then ZAP, all they find of you is a smoking ear.

I am trying to make a point here, and hope I'm succeeding. Lightning is a supreme danger that dumb consensus has happening to other people. Firefighters call those other people crispy critters, and they are not pretty, so don't be a monkey and let it happen to you. Be smart, and find suitable shelter at the first indication of a thunderstorm.

One summer, while gathering info for a mystery novel, I worked as a golf course marshal, or course ranger. I tooled around in a special golf cart speeding up slow players, stopping the odd fight and generally putting myself in harm's way for free golf. That particular course had an automatic lightning warning system that detected increased electrical fields and sounded a siren located on nearly every hole. That siren could knock squirrels out of trees, and it always astounded me that golfers couldn't hear it—they would just keep playing. Which is what I meant by harm's way, as I had to put myself into dangerous situations to order those deaf players off the course and into shelters. Did they appreciate my efforts? No, they went grumbling, complaining, threatening to get me fired, and glancing back like…monkeys. Which goes a long way to explain from where cometh my simian analogies.

The Knowing

The elders of some Canadian Aboriginal bands still maintain the ancient traditions of weather telling. Cloud shapes, wind direction, humidity, and the behaviour of certain birds, animals, insects, as well as personal insight tell them what's in store for the band. Weighed down by belongings, the Inuit today can no longer pack up sleds and mush from harm's way. First Nation bands no longer have easily pulled-down tipis, and the Métis are rooted in the social fabric.

But in the past, knowing weather was literally a matter of life and death for many bands, and their elders were so good at predicting weather that meteorologists have taken to studying and adopting their tuning-in methods. In Australia, experts are so intrigued with Aboriginal weather lore that they created a database encompassing 50,000 years of forecasting history.

WEATHER OMENS

Foretelling the Future

Small showers last long,
But sudden storms are short

–William Shakespeare, *Richard III*

This is the Bard making note of weather fronts in a military play. During Shakespeare's time, telling the weather was of vital importance to armies on the march. Neither side wanted to fight on a cold, miserable field, so battles often occurred in early spring or late fall, after planting and harvesting. In those months, weather could turn from fine to nasty in hours, so any good general would consult an "omen reader" before embarking on a campaign. Omen readers would emulate both the Venetian ship captains and the Egyptian priests; they would "feel" the weather and keep records. From those tuned-in omen readers, we get weather proverbs such as:

The first three days of a season
Rule the weather for that season

And from French omen readers we get…the weather paper. These are nothing but rag paper soaked in a solution of chloride of cobalt and then dried and cut into various designs. On dry days the paper is blue; when humidity increases to signal a storm, it changes to a lilac colour, and finally to pink. These are still made and sold all over Europe—a novelty item now, but generals of old wanting to be tuned-in, paid fortunes to own one.

What is this tuning-in method? It's stopping to smell the roses. It's looking around and taking the measure of clouds, wind speed, direction and humidity. It's all there, and you play the hunch. Anyone can do it, and with a little practice the payoff can be a lifesaver. Trust your instincts, and do not put all your faith in weather forecasters. Those people are notorious for fudging weather predictions to avoid being wrong. According to John Coleman, founder of The Weather Channel, weather forecasters have been telling us what we want to hear and not what we need to know. He claims greed has turned weather forecasting into a tool of big business with billions of dollars at stake. Coleman also argues that a big business conspiracy is manipulating the American and Canadian public into believing the earth is doomed by warming and pollution so they will accept exorbitant gas prices and carbon taxes. Believe him or not, his accusations cast doubt on an industry most people have learned to depend upon.

How can we foretell our own weather so we can walk the dog without fear of being soaked or vaporized?

WEATHER FORECASTING 101

Weather Wisdom

Buy a barometer and tap, tap. Then, while you're walking outside to check the clouds and wind direction, take stock of your physical condition. Any aches or pains absent during yesterday's fine weather? Corns or bunions hurting? A building or approaching storm will increase negatively charged moisture in the air, repelling a similar charge in the soil and luring positive ions to the surface. This is an unnatural condition for humans and causes us various aches and pains, as does changing air pressure. These can put many of us "under the weather." How's your mental state in a rainstorm? Does rain make you feel "a little blue"?

Outside, you listen. Can you hear a whispering noise? That is vegetation discharging electricity into the air, "the whispering pines." City dwellers will never hear it, but country folk know it like a friend. Those trees can tell you more; for example, if a storm is imminent, the leaves of many species (like poplars) will turn. Any country boy can tell you a silvery-looking tree means head for the barn. He also may point out that the cows are lying down, backs against the coming storm. He might tell you an old rhyme: "Tails to the east—weather's least. Tails to the west—weather's best." Or he might even tell you his father can forecast storms by listening to a train whistle. The whistle makes a different sound when bad weather is coming down the track. Yup, that's true—it's a phenomenon caused by sound travelling faster in moisture-laden air.

Next to the barometer, moisture in the air is your greatest prediction tool for weather. An approaching storm will increase humidity until saturation, and with a little practice you can learn to associate how much with how far and know exactly when the storm will arrive. Humidity is lowest during fair weather and begins increasing 6 to 12 hours before a storm. Women find storm prediction easy, as the rise in humidity will make their hair unmanageable.

Hey Martha! Your hair looks a mess. No golf today. Let's do something else.

Fog means that chances for rain are excellent. Fog is created by a temperature difference between the earth and the overlying air and means that air is super saturated. If the temp drops a bit, you better head for shelter as cooler air means less saturation. It's going to rain, dude. Better call the dog and head for the barn.

Halos around the sun or the moon are other signs of oncoming rain. The halos are ice crystals and mean warm air is rising and will soon be cooling. A small halo means you have plenty of time, while a big one means, better walk the dog now.

Clarity of vision is another sign that it will rain soon as vapour-saturated air is much more transparent than dry. At night, lights will have unusual clarity, and during the day, you'll be cancelling your appointment with the optometrist.

> *Red sky in morning, sailors take warning.*
> *Red sky at night, sailors delight.*

—Ancient sailor lore

When in the evening, ye say, it will be fair weather for the sky is red. And in the morning, it will be foul today, for the sky is red and lowering.

—Mathew 16: 2-3

A coloured sky occurs when the sun's rays are split into colours of the spectrum by the atmosphere and bounce off particulates and vapour. Since weather patterns generally move from west to east (trade winds), the ancient mariners knew a red sky meant the morning sun was illuminating weather gone by and humidity would soon rise and bring more weather. While inversely, the setting sun illuminated weather to come, usually fair since a high concentration of particulates indicates stable air. But not always, and a red sky at night probably tempted many a ship's captain to overreach, and as the English are prone to say, come a cropper.

Swallows are good storm indicators; they catch insects on the wing and imminent nasty weather will have their prey flying close to the ground. If those birds are darting about close to the ground, expect a rainstorm.

Shore birds will not fly in bad weather. If you live by the sea or a large lake and happen to sea an unusual number of gulls and plovers standing on the beach, be assured bad weather is just over the horizon.

Seagull, seagull sitting on the sand
It's never good weather when you're on land.

−Unknown

Crickets sing in tune with the temperature, and when the song changes from a trill to a chirp, it means the temp is falling and something mean lurks over the horizon. Elders of some First Nation bands are adept at reading the chirp of crickets.

Spiders desert their webs before a storm. An empty web is generally a good sign rain is on the way. If you see a spider weaving in the morning, the weather should be fair:

When spiders weave their webs by noon
Fine weather is coming soon.

−Unknown

Honeybees are sensitive to static electricity and will beeline back to the hive when they detect a rise. A nice sunny day in the garden with no bees buzzing indicates a change in the weather.

Small mammals such as raccoons, possums, squirrels and coyotes know when a storm is brewing and will head for cover. The great earthquake that shattered Indonesia in 2004 created a monster tsunami that killed 100,000 people, but no wild animals. Somehow their wild critters sensed the coming wave and made a beeline to higher ground. Indonesian authorities are still amazed by the phenomena and have established a watch agency to keep tabs on movements of wild animals. If you're smart, you'll take a page from the Indonesians and keep an eye on your own critters. If you see them heading for higher ground, better grab some lunch and go with the flow.

Domestic animals are worth watching:

> *When pigs carry sticks,*
> *The clouds will play tricks.*
> *When they lie in the mud,*
> *No fears of a flood.*

–Unknown

Most pets exhibit certain traits when a storm is approaching: cats may sneeze, dogs may scratch—"*but when the donkey blows his horn, it's time to house your wheat and corn*" (Unknown).

Flowers can protect their pollen against rain by closing blooms, and while a few cold ground species such as tulips and crocuses do that quickly, gentian will do it right before your eyes. Plant some near your front steps and give them a glance on the way out the door. Flowers shut tight means take the umbrella and leave the dog.

Dandelions will close their down when a storm threatens. The common chickweed and clover will both close up shop, and sunflower heads turning straight up is a sure sign of rain.

Be weather wise; it's so simple, and may save your life.

Weird Weather Stories

One rain does not make a crop.

–Creole proverb

METEOROLOGICAL MAYHEM

Ball of Trouble

The C-130 Hercules aircraft encountered wind shear as it flared for a landing at Resolute Bay on Elsmere Island. The giant aircraft slewed sideways, skidded the length of the runway and bellied into a pile of ice scrapings from the runway. Damage was minimal and confined to the plane's fuselage. Ice shards had pierced the aluminum skin of the aircraft, making about 50 tiny holes, and while the mechanics lacked machinery to repair those punctures, they proclaimed the Hercules flight-worthy in spite of the damage.

The plane was now a giant sieve with engines, but no matter, it could fly, and the tiny holes made for some interesting musical sounds, depending on speed and angle. At 10,000 metres,

and a few minutes after midnight on January 26, 1975, the pilots made music to accompany a light show created by the plane's four propellers slicing ion-charged, arctic air. In –50°C, air static zap comes in all colours, blue mostly, but sometimes red and yellow. Sizzling colours that reached from spinners to wings like fingers playing oversized flutes. Neat, but after a while interest waned, and the co-pilot fell asleep—arctic flights are long and taking turns was the accepted drill.

A banging noise alerted the pilot, and in the cargo hold, that meant stowaway. Closer to their destination it would have been ignored, but because they were far away from landing, it had to be investigated. The pilot eased himself from the seat, grabbed a flashlight and ducked into the huge cargo hold. He didn't need the flashlight; the "stowaway" dazzled like a kid's sparkler. A vivid orange colour, and about the size of a softball, it moved up and down like a wigwag on a railway crossing. A yell brought the co-pilot, who kept rubbing his eyes like he couldn't believe what he was seeing. It was ball lightning, mentioned tongue in cheek during pilot training, but never quite believed. Only there it was, in all its miniscule glory. It looked pretty cool, until it began bouncing around like a rubber ball. At that point, the pilots remembered that the thing could short out electronics. It must be kept from entering the flight deck, but how? There was no door. While the pilot frantically moved cargo to make a wall, the co-pilot kept shouting that the event should only be lasting a few seconds. It lasted more than five minutes, and vanished. Then it was back to business for the pilots, but not for long.

The ball returned, but this time the pilots knew from where and why it lasted so long. They had watched out the cockpit window and seen the static-like fingers snap together and spawn the ball. Interesting, but when the ball suddenly slipped through the holes in the fuselage, panic resumed. More stuff got heaved onto the barricade: jackets, life preservers, manuals, anything they could find, but the sparking ball had taken to bouncing longitudinally and entered the flight deck in spite of the wall. Had it gone right through the cases? The pilots weren't sure, but thinking three's a crowd, one made a desperate grab at the throttles and pulled them straight back. With four engines coughing and sputtering, and both pilots fearing the worst, the sparking ball made an exit through a window, leaving the pilots with a good story to tell their grandchildren.

World War II pilots called these glowing balls "foo-fighters" and saw a lot of them. Scientists claimed they were drops of engine oil turned into molten plasma by static electricity. Later, they would say the same thing about foo-fighter sightings by jet pilots, completely ignoring the fact that those aircraft used no oil.

Ball lightning exists, but occurs so infrequently that studying them is impossible, and they continue to baffle scientists. Go online and you will find instructions for making your own foo ball in a microwave oven. Should you happen upon an au natural, be advised that while C-130 Hercules aircraft do have two hinged flight deck windows, all were closed tight because of the cold, and that foo ball made its exit through some very thick glass.

The Wind and Mr. Bell

Although the telephone is not entirely a Canadian invention, because Alexander Graham Bell lived in Boston, Massachusetts, when he perfected the device, the idea is all ours. That eureka moment burst from his bean while on a visit to his parents' house in Brantford, Ontario, where he had gone to escape the oppressive heat of a Boston summer. He would always tell reporters, "My telephone was conceived in Brantford, and born in Boston."

Bell, a naturalized American citizen from Scotland who answered to the name Alec his whole life, only perfected the device. Antonio Meucci, a poor Italian immigrant who received no remuneration or recognition for such a fabulous discovery, did the actual inventing. But that's another story, as this one concerns Alec Bell, the winds of Nova Scotia and something he really did invent, the airplane. Surprised? You probably thought the Wright brothers at Kitty Hawk in 1903 were the first to fly a heavier-than-air aircraft. That's the American mindset, and nothing could be further from the truth.

In 1848, an Englishman, John Stringfellow, strapped a small steam engine onto a glider and flew several hundred metres. In 1853, another Englishman, Sir George Caley, ordered his coachman into a fixed wing glider and sent him off on a flight of several hundred metres. A few years later, in 1857, two Frenchmen, Felix Du Temple and his brother Louis, stuck a pair of small steam engines onto a monoplane glider, took off, flew a short distance, and landed safely. After the French success, a whole series of aviators took to the skies, and their accomplishments were significant steps towards perfection.

The Wrights' feat at Kitty Hawk was simply a few more rungs up a long ladder. As the 19th century ended, anxiety among daredevil glider pilots grew; coach and bicycle manufacturers had already fixed gasoline engines to their creations and powered flight had become almost a reality. The race was on, and the participants legion. Hundreds of ornithopters, helicopters, mono and multi-winged gliders got powered up and smashed by overeager participants with little or no understanding of what it took to get a machine airborne. The few who did get into the air came a cropper because their aircraft lacked controls; what goes up comes down hard without control surfaces. The Wright brothers understood this and spent years perfecting ways to control their glider, and while they were doing this, Alec Bell put aside the telephone and began experimenting with kites.

In 1896, Bell had settled into his newly built Nova Scotia mansion, and while the Wrights were still fixing bicycles, Samuel Pierpoint Langley placed a gasoline motor on an unmanned glider and sent it flying a half-mile down Washington's Potomac River. Aviation historians consider that flight the first for a heavier-than-air aircraft, and it so impressed the U.S. government they gave Langley $50,000 to build a piloted aircraft. Wanting that done faster, the Smithsonian Institute added another $20,000, setting off a chain of events that eventually led Bell and the Smithsonian to become involved in a game of fraud and duplicity. Interesting stuff, but what does it have to do with weather?

Flying has everything to do with weather; Alec Bell knew this from watching gulls fly in a stiff wind. Gulls attacked the air, and with his gift for perfecting, Bell knew power was the key to controlled flight. Sam Langley's engineer, a man called Charles Manly, had perfected a rotary engine with plenty of power, and Bell had no doubt Langley's plane, the Great

Aerodrome, would be the first heavier-than-air controlled flyer. At the beginning of 1903 Langley launched his powered gliders twice and failed both times. A few months later the Wrights flew at Kitty Hawk, a feat both Bell, the Smithsonian and half the world failed to acknowledge. The Smithsonian, to which Bell had been elected a regent in 1898, went so far as to display Langley's plane, labelling it the first heavier-than-air aircraft. Convinced the Wrights' under-powered (12-horsepower), droopy winged aircraft had been lofted by wind and their flight just a long glide, Bell threw himself into the fray. By 1907 he had several aircraft designed and formed the Arial Experiment Association (AEA) to get them airborne. The association had five members, Alec Bell, two University of Toronto engineering graduates J.A.D. McCurdy and Fredrick W. Baldwin, an American army lieutenant, Thomas Selfridge, and the fastest man alive, the American motorcycle manufacturer Glenn H. Curtiss.

The next year, 1908, the AEA moved to Hammondsport, New York, and began flying aircraft with powerful engines, enclosed cockpits, control yokes and Bell's perfected inventions, tricycle landing gear and ailerons. Ailerons are small wings at the end of the wings that control bank, or roll, about an aircraft's longitudinal axis. They made turning easier, safer and put the AEA planes a cut above Wright-designed aircraft. The Wright brothers were continuously crashing planes, while the AEA made over 150 flights with no mishaps. In 1909, the group moved back to Nova Scotia and flew their ultimate design, the Silver Dart, the first modern airplane. Now master of wind and sky, Bell turned to other interests, and the AEA moved into the history books.

The following is an aside, because I know you're dying to learn about the fraud and duplicity.

After the dissolution of the AEA, Bell gave the Silver Dart design to McCurdy, Baldwin and Glenn Curtiss. McCurdy and Baldwin formed the Canadian Aerodrome Company and began selling planes to the military. Curtiss formed the Curtiss Aircraft Company and began demonstrating aircraft to interested parties in competition with the Wright brothers who held a patent on heavier-than-air aircraft. Curtiss offered a superior aircraft, and to put him out of business, the Wrights sued.

Alec Bell, regent of the Smithsonian, and Sam Langley, the Institute's secretary, hatched a plan to defeat the Wrights' lawsuit and promote the Smithsonian's claim that Langley's aircraft, the Great Aerodrome, was the first heavier-than-air controlled aircraft. If they could get the Great Aerodrome to fly, their lawyers claimed they could get the Wrights' patent disallowed. So it was, in the beginning months of 1914, they dispatched Glenn Curtiss to examine Great Aerodrome for airworthiness. He reported the plane would never fly unless he made changes to the design, an illegal undertaking. His partners agreed, and Curtiss made the changes behind closed doors. The redesigned Langley plane made a short flight, but failed to impress the courts. The Wrights' patent held, but the big lie supplied lawyers with a reason to appeal, and the case dragged on while Curtiss continued selling airplanes. Years of legal battles ensued, until the surviving Wright brother, Orville, tired of the fight and lost interest in the case. In 1929, the Wright Aeronautical Corporation and the Curtiss Aeroplane Company merged to form the Curtiss-Wright Corporation that survives to this day.

The Punch Redux

In the early hours of December 2, 2008, pilots Curtis Peters and Tom Hinderk nosed a tiny Kelly-D replica biplane onto a runway at the Calgary airport and readied for takeoff. Curtis turned around and stared at his co-pilot. He was looking for second thoughts, because taking off into the wild blue in an open cockpit aircraft in the dead of winter seemed an insane undertaking. The temperature was –17°C, and the prop wash made it feel more like –40°C, and they were still on the ground. Curtis saw Tom smile and jerk a thumb into the air to signify his full commitment in recreating C.W. "Punch" Dickens first airmail flight between Calgary and Edmonton. Curtis nodded, and turning back to the controls, eased the throttle forward, sending the Kelly-D biplane barrelling down the runway. The old bird might look old, but a brand-new Lycoming engine put the tiny, fabric-covered aircraft at 3000 metres in minutes. Cold on the ground had now become bone-snapping brutal with a nasty head wind. Uttering a little prayer of thanks for his battery-heated socks and special facemask, Curtis aimed the little plane west. He thought about the old days, those days he and Tom were emulating, when at 11:00 AM, on November 11, 1918, the Great War in Europe ground to a halt and a half million of Canada's young men began trickling back to the nation's cities. They were looking to continue their lives with good jobs. Only, wartime production had stopped, and paying jobs in the eastern provinces were scarce.

Soldiers returning to the western provinces fared little better, as lack of demand had caused grain prices to plummet along with opportunities. Some westerners returned to school, most to the family farm, while a few, employing talents they learned overseas, jumped on the automotive bandwagon. Military engineers turned to building roads and bridges, mechanics opened gas stations, and cooks operated roadside

diners. Canada had become a nation on wheels, and opportunities abounded for soldiers able to repair and service cars
and trucks.

Wartime production had also created opportunities for another
cadre of returning heroes…the pilots. Military aircraft production had ceased, and surplus airplanes could be picked up
cheap by those who could fly them. Ace pilots like Ernie Hoy,
who on August 7, 1919, made the first airmail flight over the
Canadian Rockies flying a surplus Curtiss JN-4—a historic
flight from Vancouver to Calgary that lasted 16 hours and
42 minutes. There were also fliers like Calgary native Freddy
McCall, who bought surplus planes and went barnstorming
across the West taking people aloft for a fee.

Edmonton native and war ace Wilfrid "Wop" May returned
to rent a Curtiss JN-4 from the City of Edmonton, and from
the Sproule Farm on that city's outskirts operated Canada's
first registered aircraft company, May Airplanes Ltd.

Also returning to Edmonton were Captain Keith Tailyour and Jock MacNeill who collaborated in January 1920 to form The Edmonton Aircraft Company on a leased section of farmland owned by the Hagmann family, a site now occupied by the Edmonton Municipal Airport.

By 1926, the Hagmann's cow pasture had become Blatchford Field, complete with runways and hangers, and it was this—ready for the future modernization—that caused James Richardson, a hugely successful grain merchant, to buy 12 brand-new Fokker Standard airplanes and found Western Canadian Airways. Then came Lindbergh's solo flight across the Atlantic in May 1927 and things changed. Pilots suddenly became celebrities, and men of the Royal Flying Corps slung the white silk around their necks and began flying again.

One of the first pilots hired by Richardson's new air venture was Edmonton native and war ace, C.W. "Punch" Dickens, a man with an eye to the future of mail delivery.

On December 10, 1928, Punch flew into the history books by driving an open cockpit airplane full of mail from a scrubby field outside Winnipeg, Manitoba, to Blatchford Field in Edmonton. It was the city's first airmail delivery, and although the 1300-kilometre trip does not sound like much of an event, it was, for its time, a physical and technological triumph deserving of a modern-day redux.

An opportunity presented to the Alberta Aviation Museum in Edmonton by the estate of a Winnipeg aircraft enthusiast—a fabric-covered, open cockpit Kelly-D biplane, a modern-day replica of the same type of airplane Punch had flown to deliver the first mail. Who would be crazy enough to fly that aircraft in the dead of winter, when temperatures aloft can dip to –30°C and brutal winds can make it feel more like –50°C?

Curtis laughed, thinking of he and Tom almost falling over themselves for the chance to emulate Punch Dickens.

Now thinking of the three days that lay ahead, Curtis slapped his mitts while searching the horizon for their first stop, Neepawa, Manitoba. Cursing the bitter cold, he heard Tom yell through the intercom that they should have worn white silk scarves so they could repair holes in the fabric should they run into hail. Curtis had thought of many things, but not that, and his laugh rippled through the plane like a shiver.

With both pilots freezing cold, but happy, the little plane began a gentle descent towards Neepawa where a roaring fire and bowls of hot soup awaited the intrepid voyagers. Their flight was on time and proceeding according to schedule. Tomorrow they would fly to Russell, Manitoba, and Yorkton, Saskatchewan; the next day to Saskatoon, and the next to Lloydminster and Edmonton. Only 80 kilometres of short hops; what could possibly go wrong?

The going wrong began that night in the midnight hours. Freezing rain, and in the morning our intrepid heroes found the hanger protecting their aircraft sealed like an icy tomb. The hanger doors would not budge, and when the ice finally relented to axe and hammer, it was too late to fly. No problem, they would take off the next morning, weather permitting.

It did not permit, and foul weather kept the plane on the ground while Curtis and Tom commuted back and forth from Edmonton, ever hopeful. Twice they braved marginal weather and took off, only to find headwinds that could make their little biplane fly backwards.

On their third try, in ideal flying conditions, their plane suffered electrical problems and needed repairs. Tom and Curtis continued their commutes, still confident, while others were thinking the redux cursed and that Edmonton would never see the Kelly-D biplane.

On January 19, 2009, a Monday morning with sunny skies, Curtis taxied the plane onto the runway at Neepawa. There was no turning back; this was make it or break it time. Make it they did, but their overnight at Yorkton featured a fitful sleep due to an unfavourable wind report.

The report was on the money, and Tuesday's flight to Saskatoon took seven hours instead of four, and in –50°C temperatures. Hauling their frozen bodies from the aircraft in Saskatoon, Tom told reporters, "There's a reason why guys aren't flying open cockpit biplanes in the wintertime anymore."

Wednesday morning dawned bright and clear with no serious wind problems. Did this mean the curse had lifted? Curtis and Tom headed skywards to find out. Reaching 1000 metres they could see Edmonton on the horizon; they were going to make it, no problem. Only three more stops and they were home free: North Battleford, Lloydminster and Vegreville.

Those short hops went by without a hitch, and convinced the curse was now history, the pilots lifted the tiny plane off the Vegreville runway for the short flight to Edmonton. Relieved, Curtis grabbed his radio microphone to contact Edmonton control for landing instructions. "Edmonton tower, this is the Kelly-D of the Calgary to Edmonton commemorative flight. I am inbound for landing."

Curtis waited, expecting a welcome home and landing instructions, only his radio remained silent. He tried again, and still nothing. With a glance back at Tom, Curtis began circling the tiny aircraft within sight of the control tower. A dead radio meant the curse had not gone away, but their circling brought help from an aircraft belonging to the Civil Air Search and Rescue Association and a guide to a safe landing.

End of story, but maybe not, as plans have been made to send the plane on another Wop May redux, his famous 1929 mercy flight to northern Alberta, where he and co-pilot Vic Horner delivered diphtheria vaccine in the dead of winter. Volunteers, anyone...anyone?

The Windy Movie Critic

Thorold, Ontario, is a sleepy little town near Niagara Falls. Not much to do in Thorold, but they do have a four-screen drive-in theatre. On the evening of May 20, 1996, the movie *Twister* was the feature film.

Hey, Martha, get the kids ready. We'll go early and get right up front.

Grudgingly, she piled the kids into the car and off they drove thinking of popcorn, candy and hot dogs. Dad had the big drive-in marquee in sight when the kids started laughing, pointing and asking how they made it look so real. Dad turned to look, saw a funnel cloud churning up the field next to them, and lost control of his bladder. Horrified, he slammed on the brakes and watched a skinny tornado move onto the road and head for the drive-in.

Ten minutes later, with everything looking quiet, Dad once again headed for the drive-in, only to find it had become a three-screen establishment and his movie selection cancelled. The small tornado had made off with the screen slated to show the tornado movie *Twister*.

The next day, newspapers all over the U.S. and Canada printed the story but blew it all out of proportion. According to their articles, the packed drive-in had *Twister* running when the tornado struck. They even had quotes from people who claimed they watched the tornado tear up the screen and thought it a promotional stunt. Yellow journalism, but still a weird event.

The Wandering Cottage

Big living room, three bedrooms, and a screened porch with an unobstructed view of Lake Erie. Sounds pretty nice, but when my grandfather happened onto that cottage in 1928 while on a day trip to Port Ryerse, Ontario, it was flotsam.

The night before his visit, a violent thunderstorm had rolled down the lake pushing up water like a bulldozer. Lake Erie had exploded onto the Port Ryerse beach, plucking dozens of cottages off their foundations. While most of them had disintegrated, the cottage my granddad found had floated a kilometre or so down the beach and nestled onto the shore as if it belonged there. My granddad took a liking to that well-built cottage and even helped the owner in the recovery project. And for that, when the telephone rang three years later, he recognized the excited voice telling him the same thing had happened to the cottage and would he like to buy the flotsam.

My granddad readily agreed, and remembering the three strikes rule, had the cottage moved off the beach and onto a hill, the highest point in Port Ryerse. It's still there, looking like it belongs, but the view of Lake Erie from the screened porch is completely obstructed by trees.

The Vanishing Pigeons

Port Ryerse, Ontario, was a bustling lake port during the 19th century with all manner of goods being shipped out to the U.S. and Britain: lumber, bricks, pottery, live hogs, fresh fish and barrels of salted pigeons. That's right, pigeons. Every spring, huge flocks of passenger pigeons were driven across Lake Erie by storms, darkening the skies over Port Ryerse while residents netted, shot or knocked them down with bamboo poles.

All that changed in 1867 when the pigeons arrived in only small numbers. Local lore has an American hurricane blowing the migrating birds out to sea, and this could be true. In that year, the fifth-worst hurricane in U.S. history tore up the east coast on June 22, well ahead of normal hurricane season and directly in the migration path of those millions of pigeons

But while the eastern flocks of pigeons dwindled, farther west, millions of the birds still moved north in the spring. They did that without fail until the spring of 1886, when only one bird arrived at the nesting grounds near Lake Superior.

It's a mystery what happened to those millions of birds; historians blame overhunting, loss of habitat or disease. But 1886 saw an outbreak of tornadoes in the American Midwest, dozens of them, including the great F4 Sauk Rapids tornado that ripped through Minnesota, killing 30 people and injuring hundreds—tornadoes that would have been directly in the flight path of those migrating pigeons.

Note: In mid-November 1999, a large flock of cliff swallows were observed in New Brunswick. Since swallows migrate from there to the Caribbean in late August, it's theorized those birds were pushed over 1600 kilometres north by the winds of Hurricane Gert. Swallows know to bend with the wind and let it carry them along, while the now extinct passenger pigeons, like schooling fish, depended on shear numbers for protection.

The Rubber Ducky Chronicle

The captain of the container ship stared at the radar repeater while swivelling his chair back and forth like a nervous tic. The 1992 typhoon season had just begun and trouble loomed on the horizon, an unexpected area of low pressure showed as a large, bright green blob on the radar display. It indicated a bad storm that looked too large to skirt. He would have to sail his ship straight through and hope his deck cargo stayed put. His vessel hauled over 5000 containers stacked six high over the main deck and looked top heavy. Only she wasn't, and the captain had every confidence his ship could weather any storm. It was the deck cargo that bothered him—the stacks he could barely see over were placed into sockets at their four corners and depended on weight to hold them in place. He could only hope they had put heavier containers on top. He knew over 10,000 containers a year jumped ship in rough seas, but he had never lost one. Turning to his helmsman, who steered the ship electronically but still kept the name, the captain ordered him to override his computer and keep the ship's bow heading into the waves. Proper seamanship, but wandering off course and using extra fuel would take a lot of explaining to the ship owners in Hong Kong. They ran ships for profit and cared nothing about seamanship, and if containers broke loose, so what, that's why they paid the insurance company. Looking defeated, the captain turned back to the helmsman and countermanded his order. They would steam straight through and hope for the best.

Night fell just as the storm arrived and huge waves beset the vessel from every direction except head on the bow. The captain didn't sleep a wink, and if he did doze a few minutes, thoughts of his cargo slipping into the deep soon had him wide awake. So it was a very tired-looking captain that walked from the elevator into the bridge at first light to ask about any missing containers. His first mate, looking pleased with himself, reported that only 12 forty-footers had gone AWOL.

The captain, however, was not pleased; 12 wasn't bad, considering all the rock and roll, but his perfect record was down the drain, and when the first mate laughed, it was all he could do to keep from punching the guy. Instead, he asked what was so funny, and got shown a video for reply. The bridge watch had seen the containers fly off and with nothing better to do had turned on the big lights to watch for more deserters. When no more containers fell overboard, they turned the lights onto the sea and grabbed the camera to film what the captain was watching. At this point in the video both the captain, the first mate and three others on the bridge broke out laughing. Crushed by water pressure as they sank, the containers had released their contents, and in the video, those contents jumped from the sea like luminescent popcorn. Small toys popped up by the thousands until they covered the raging sea like a blanket: yellow ducks, green frogs, bright red beavers and luminescent blue turtles.

Upon reaching his port of destination, Tacoma, Washington, and curious about the tub toys, the captain inquired and learned there'd been 29,000 of the little guys. Thinking of that comical flotilla sailing off on a great adventure brought a smile to his face, but when handed a telephone number and told someone wanted to speak to him about the tub toys, the smile disappeared. An insurance adjuster maybe, but when he called the number, the man who answered was Curtis Ebbesmeyer, a Seattle-based oceanographer. Ebbesmeyer wanted to know what the tub toys looked like and if they had any brand names or numbers. Asking why, the captain learned that Curtis had been tracking marine flotsam around the world since 1990, when the container ship *Hansa Carrier* lost a cargo of 80,000 Nike sneakers and work boots. The boots and shoes all had individual registration numbers and it had immediately occurred to Curtis, who was studying ocean currents in the northeast Pacific, that these would make wonderful current markers. The sneakers were already out there, and they were a whole lot cheaper than the bottles and yellow tags he'd been using. Intrigued, the captain agreed to obtain and send him the tub toy information.

Six months later, Ebbesmeyer once again contacted the captain with news that some of his tub toy flotilla had been found on a beach in Sitka, Alaska, more than 3500 kilometres from where they entered the ocean.

They agreed to meet, and that afternoon, over a coffee at Starbucks, the captain heard for the first time about the Great Pacific Garbage Dump. He had asked where the tub toys would eventually wind up, and having already visualized the flotilla heading for exotic beaches, was surprised to hear they were destined to float back and forth between Japan and the U.S. mainland. Ebbesmeyer explained that the lost cargo of toys had gone into a rotating current called the North Pacific Subtropical Gyre. They would spend their existence travelling in a 10,943-kilometre circle along with countless other pieces of plastic flotsam and garbage as everything that floats in the northern Pacific ends up in the Subtropical Gyre, a purgatory for plastics and a giant garbage dump. Now and then, a wind change will blow some onto beaches all up and down the coast, and for that he formed his loose-knit organization of beachcombers. It was an idea he got after learning that beachcombers were having meetings to exchange washed-up Nike sneakers.

Fun and games, but Ebbesmeyer had a deadly serious reason for wanting to map the currents of the Gyre. A plastic object

will break down eventually, but its molecules hang around forever and mix with seawater to form a thick soup of plastic dust that Ebbesmeyer fears is winding up in the food chain.

Life goes on, and for a dozen years the captain sailed, Ebbesmeyer plotted currants, and the Subtropical Gyre gathered in floaters. But one day, after docking his ship in Tacoma and hopping a cab into the city, the captain heard a startling bit of news on the cab's radio; a military aircraft flying south of Greenland had spotted a brightly coloured mass floating on the ocean's surface. Going down for a closer look, the crew of the aircraft determined the mass was actually a flotilla of plastic tub toys. Laughing, the captain listened to how his toys had made an impossible journey through the Northwest Passage entering the Atlantic near Greenland. His tub toys had jumped ship, escaped the Gyre, traversed the Arctic, and would arrive somewhere on the coast of Ireland or Scandinavia sometime that summer.

That night, at his hotel, the captain ordered a glass of champagne with dinner and offered up a toast to his adventurous cargo of tub toys.

Note: At this writing, a few tubs toys have washed up on British beaches, but the majority entered the gulf stream and are headed for Nova Scotia. The First Years, the American company that ordered the tub toys, is offering a reward for any found toys carrying their logo, and collectors on eBay will bid large for yellow ducks.

Weather Modification

What this country needs is more people to inspire others with confidence and fewer people to discourage any initiative in the right direction, more to get into the thick of things and fewer to sit on the sidelines merely finding fault, more to point out what's right with the world and fewer to keep harping on what's wrong with it.

–Father James Keller

THE TRAVELLING MEDICINE SHOW

Weather Wizards

From 1840 to the 1930s, coaxing rain from stubborn skies was the part-time job of the travelling medicine man and his colourful snake oil show. Forerunners of the travelling circus, these guys crisscrossed rural America and Canada putting on shows and hawking alcohol-laced patent medicines to a stressed population who was ready and willing to buy any form of temporary relief. Scraping a living from the ground was hard work and, without irrigation, a financially precarious undertaking. Farmers planted crops, prayed for rain and even hired people to help them pray, people like the travelling medicine man.

It was like *The Rainmaker* movie, because drought opened doors for unscrupulous medicine men. Farmers bought their elixirs, and maybe they would buy their rain too? A ludicrous idea, but medicine men had big imaginations and were as adept at reading the weather as Venetian sea captains. They knew when to stay and when to start a journey, and some sought to profit on that ability. They would roll their wagons into a drought-stricken area and hang around outside a town until weather conditions looked about right for a rainfall, and then out would come the big rainmaker banner.

The deal was a community affair; the rainmaker guaranteed to produce rain in six days (God rested one day) for "x" number of dollars or it would not cost the community a red cent. A good deal all around, especially for the medicine man who sold his elixirs, and if his cloud reading proved correct, got a bonus.

Not bad, but nobody got rich, not until the newspapers discovered the *Storm King*, James Pollard Espy. In 1841, Espy wrote a book, *The Philosophy of Storms,* in which he laid out in print his discoveries and observations of the mechanics of thunderstorms and how stubborn weather systems could be induced to precipitate by introducing soot particulates into updrafts. Espy cited the observations of Benjamin Matthias of Philadelphia, who on repeated visits to English industrial cities noticed that it rained every day except for Sundays, when the factories shut down. Espy theorized that carbon particulates from industrial pollution acted as a catalyst to promote rainfall, a theory he attempted to sell to the U.S. Congress as a way to keep the Ohio River open to summertime navigation.

It was a dud deal with Congress, but Espy's book became a hit with those imaginative travelling medicine men, who immediately began using various and sundry polluting devices to seed clouds. The newspapers of the day loved James Pollard Espy and called him the father of modern American meteorology. Pure sensationalism, but it lent credence to rainmaking, and it became a semi-respected occupation. Neat, but still nobody got rich. Not until 1848, when something happened to change the fortunes of rainmakers; gold was discovered in California and a lot of opportunistic folks moved westward.

The Show Moves West

But, what has gold in California got to do with Canada?

Plenty, because in those days the border was just an imaginary line, and when 300,000 people suddenly stampeded west to find their fortunes in the gold fields, a good percentage of those stampeding were Canadians. The fact is, for the remainder of the 19th century, Canada was an immigration conduit to the American West.

Europeans streamed into Montréal and worked their way to Kansas City and the Oregon Trail, or to Iowa and the Diamond Trail. These trails were of great importance to Canada as they afforded our prairie settlers and people headed for the West Coast a way around the cranky Blackfoot, a First Nation people with a "me no call, you no come" attitude who inadvertently turned James Pollard Espy's rainmaking theory into a practiced fact.

Hey, Martha! This guy has me confused. What do those Blackfoot people have to do with rainmaking?

The answer is…they burned prairie grasslands big time. Every year the Blackfoot torched huge tracts of prairie grass to promote new growth and attract buffalo. That it always rained during these burnings was a phenomenon not missed by the Espy-reading, ever-roaming snake oil men. The medicine men quickly emulated the Blackfoot technique and burned stuff, a lot of stuff: forests, prairie grass, haystacks and woodpiles. Stuff went up in smoke all over the Midwest, doubling the rainmakers' successes and turning some into very wealthy men.

In the early 20th century, rainmakers found Canada a lucrative stomping ground—the railway was complete, and World War I had tripled the price of wheat. Large farms sprang up everywhere; however, Canadian farmers would have no part of burning prairie land, forcing the rainmakers to use large vessels called smudge pots that produced soot (carbon particulates). This filthy but notable invention was also useful in suppressing frost and fog and was manufactured commercially right up to the 1960s.

How effective were these rainmakers? Estimates vary, but five percent is a safe bet, and usually confined to a small area and of very short duration. But it worked, some of the time, and that caught the attention of the Canadian government, which began a series of on and off testing of carbon particulate–induced rainmaking right up to November 1946. That month, an American scientist, Dr. Bernard Vonnegut (author Kurt Vonnegut's brother), discovered that dry ice and silver iodide crystals were superior seeding materials. Since then, because weather modification is profitable and could be a weapon of mass destruction, businessmen and the military have suborned the part-time occupation of the medicine man/rainmaker.

TECHNOLOGICAL ADVANCES IN RAINMAKING

Do-it-yourself Rainmaking

Is rainmaking a viable science? Does it really work?

During the early '60s, a rainmaking project called Operation Umbrella began in the Lac Saint-Jean area of Québec, a region that was experiencing long-term drought conditions. The sun always shone in Lac Saint-Jean, but during the few years of Operation Umbrella, it rained almost every day. It rained so much that concerned mothers in the area petitioned the Québec government to supply them with vitamin D to protect their children from rickets, a disease caused by lack of sunshine. Newspapers picked up the story and vilified the Québec government for raining chemicals down on helpless children. Horrified of political repercussions, the Québec Minister of Natural Resources ordered a stop to all rainmaking activities in the province. That politically inspired edict put a cross-country damper on federal and provincial funding for weather-modification projects for years, except in Alberta, where experiments continued until the late '80s, when the ball got handed off to private firms.

Weather modification works, but at best only about 20 percent of the time. Not perfect by a long shot, but a whole lot better than the travelling medicine man's five percent, and being able to modify weather can be a lifesaver for drought-stricken farms and ranches. Modern cloud seeders use computers to read clouds and special aircraft to introduce a cooling medium, such as dry ice, or a nuclei-providing chemical like silver iodide that is sometimes mixed with other chemicals, such as barium.

The nuclei process is simple enough—they replicate snowflakes, and most rain starts out as snowflakes. Pilots introduce nuclei chemicals into the cloud at just the right altitude, water vapour freezes to the nuclei and a crystallized snowflake drops into warmer, lower altitudes, melting into rain before striking the ground.

China, a big believer in weather modification, spends about $100 million annually on projects and has assigned some 30,000 scientists to do research and experiments. The country also uses 7000 artillery guns and 4000 rocket launchers in cloud-seeding efforts nationwide. They have enjoyed some success, along with causing a few problems. One problem occurred in 2007 while the Chinese were engaged in pre-Olympic practice to mitigate weather, and the story was printed in China's English-language newspaper, *The China Daily*. It reported that three government planes carrying 30 technicians had flown for three hours over Inner Mongolia, dropping silver iodide and small amounts of diatomaceous earth (the skeletal remains of tiny, ancient sea creatures composed mainly of silica) into the atmosphere at about 8000 metres. Some hours later, Beijing experienced a period of extraordinary thunderstorms and suffered extensive damage. Politically unable to point fingers, the article left readers to make the connection.

Weather modification works, but there are inherent problems, control being only one. Did seeding clouds in Mongolia cause damaging storms in Beijing? Perhaps, but it can also work the opposite way, inducing rainfall in Mongolia could deprive Beijing area farmers of precipitation. Dangerous stuff, but there are presently over 150 weather-modification projects running in over 140 countries.

HAIL MODIFICATION

Damage Control

Canada is currently funding a 2008 hail-modification project in Alberta, but it's a bit of Johnny come lately, as a group of Canadian insurance companies calling themselves the Alberta Severe Weather Management Society (ASWMS) have been running the Alberta Hail Suppression Project (AHSP) for almost two decades. The success of this project is dramatic and responsible for a 50-percent reduction in hail insurance rates for Alberta farmers and ranchers, an annual savings of almost $50 million per year—a big deal for hard-pressed grain farmers.

Hail is most common in mid-latitude areas such as Alberta during summer, when surface temperatures are warm enough to create the water vapour and convective activity necessary for thunderstorms, but the higher atmosphere is still cool enough to support the formation of ice. Evaporated surface water is carried aloft by warm, rising air, and reaches cooler, higher altitudes, condensing into water droplets. Caught in strong updrafts, the droplets rise above the freezing level, where they become super cooled. During the summer months, dust is more prevalent and can be sucked into high, cold altitudes by updrafting altocumulus clouds to become hail-forming nuclei.

Alberta is called Hail Alley, and damages to crops by hail average over $100 million a year and can sometimes be much more. During the summer of 1991 a single hailstorm caused almost half a billion dollars in crop damage, so little wonder Alberta is on the forefront of weather modification.

STORM CHASING

Tracking Twisters

Chasing after tornado-generating super cells has become something of a sport. All over the American Midwest, and part of Canada, chasers zip from county to county hoping to come face-to-face with a monster wind. From May to September, the back roads of America's Midwest and Canada's prairie provinces can be crowded with thrill seekers and tornado paparazzi hoping to capture and sell video footage to TV networks. Tour operations have even sprung up to cater to those folks, and a few are successful. Only it's not all fun and games; storm chasing is serious business to meteorological scientists who want to map the idiosyncrasies of twisters and make more accurate predictions of where and when they will occur.

Up until 1985, scientists employed a heavy cylinder loaded with measuring instruments to track tornadoes. Called TOTO, for TOtable Tornado Observatory, the cylinder was strapped to the bed of a pick-up truck and dumped off into the path of a twister. That was the idea, but its weight caused problems, and it never lived up to expectations. In the 1996 Hollywood film *Twister,* chasers employed a similar device they called Dorothy that released dozens of tiny measuring instruments once the tornado had been overrun. A bit of fiction, since the real cylinder, TOTO, was designed to withstand the battering and not release anything.

In 1985, scientists at the Los Alamos National Laboratory designed a portable Doppler radar device, and things began looking up for the storm-chasing scientists. They could now get a real-time peek inside a twister. These portable Doppler units, called DOW, short for Doppler on Wheels, are mounted onto the back of pick-up trucks and stay there; they don't have to be dumped. Scientists park the truck a kilometre or two from a likely super cell, anchor the vehicle to the ground and wait for the twister to appear. If a funnel cloud develops, they fire radar beams into the monster at different angles and heights to produce a 3D image.

TOTO was now history, and the scientific instruments it carried were miniaturized and either sent aloft in weather balloons or placed inside small, lead-weighted containers called turtles. These containers resemble large overturned salad bowls, or turtles, and contain temperature and pressure gauges and are laid directly in a twister's path.

Weather balloons are floated high into the atmosphere and carry instruments aloft to gather information about super cells: air pressure, temperature and humidity.

Utilizing the DOW, scientists now had the whirling beast in 3D, but it wasn't enough, they needed a 360-degree look around, and for that they developed the mobile mesonet. Mobile mesonet is a fleet of computer-connected cars equipped with rooftop measuring instruments that drive to positions around a twister and form a net. With 3D, and 360 degrees, all researchers needed was a peek inside. For that they borrowed specially equipped and strengthened aircraft used for hurricane research and took measurements from top to bottom.

Was the picture complete? Do scientists now have a complete understanding of the whirling monster? The answer is no, because unlocking some secrets led to other, more complex questions. But the scientific chasers are still attacking, and some day the beast will be all figured out and more accurate predictions made available.

The same Doppler radar units employed by storm chasers are now used by government agencies in the U.S., Canada, Mexico and the Caribbean to provide early warning of tornadic events.

It's a network called NEXRAD (short for NEXt-generation RADar), and both researchers and the public can access the images and information online.

Spotting Tornadoes

In a supercell storm there is often, but not always, an underlying cloud rotation called a mesocyclone that can sometimes spawn twisters. But normally, when conditions are right, this mesocyclone will begin to spin and move slowly to the rear of the storm. As it moves, a large, rudder-shaped cloud drops down and may also begin to rotate—this is the wall cloud, and from here will come the most funnels. On occasions, multiple funnels will form in the wall cloud, and while most never touch ground, multiples will sometimes join up and make that connection.

After the funnel forms, bad things start happening: the already strong wind picks up speed, hailstones drop, and in the rear of the storm, behind the mesocyclone, a strong downdraft starts pounding the ground. This is the RDF, or rear flank downdraft, and it can smash houses, blow up barns, and toss cars around like toys, but it's nothing like a twister. Chasers call this area the "bear cage" and take special measures to avoid being overrun by its nastiness—a double nastiness should a tornado suddenly spawn from the mesocyclone. That's right, twisters spawn at the rear of supercell storms and can sometimes do that in a clearing sky. People think the storm has gone by, and out of the blue comes this giant twister.

Now that the rotating funnel cloud has switched into a higher gear, the rotation is faster and closer to the ground—then it suddenly narrows and reaches for ground. A twister is born and begins chewing up the countryside. Only it's not that main funnel doing the damage; it's the suction vortices, small funnels spinning around the main funnel and sucking like vacuum cleaners. These things have the strongest winds, and we owe their identification to the scientific storm chasers. Who would have guessed tornadoes would have little helpers?

Not all mesocyclones spawn funnels, and not all spawned funnel clouds become tornadoes. This is a hugely disappointing phenomenon for many adrenaline-charged storm chasers, and it's this "some do and some don't" that puzzles scientists. They have theories, but have yet to determine exactly what forces cause only some mesocyclones to spawn twisters.

But even when scientists get that and many other whirly questions figured out, and super accurate warnings become available, it won't amount to a hill of beans if people in tornado-prone areas do nothing to prepare for an event. Don't be a monkey—if storm clouds are on the horizon, keep your radio or TV tuned to a local weather service and know the difference between tornado watch and a tornado warning. "Warning" is the key word here, as they are issued only when a twister is spotted on the ground.

Conclusions

I hope you have arrived at some conclusions, like weird weather happening now has happened before and will keep happening, people should be tossed in jail for polluting, there are too many people on this planet, and the green-for-dollars doomsayers are working our population like puppets. But who are these climate doomsayers, and what are they up to anyway?

CLIMATE DOOMSAYERS

Weather Issues

Some of the climate doomsayers are an expanded population of the religious fanatics who in times gone by occupied street corners spouting end-of-the-world dogma. Some are good people who used to chain themselves to trees and roar about in rubber rafts trying to save whales, but most are people who have made good jobs for themselves. Ecology is a huge financial bandwagon with room for all kinds of agendas.

One of their favourites is carbon tax, an easy sell to both politicians and corporate polluters alike. It's knee-jerk grandstanding for politicians, and something the green-for-money gang can crow over. But it's just another tax, when what we need from our legislators is action. We need them to outlaw plastic shopping bags, three-hour fire logs, non-returnable bottles, gas lawn mowers, leaf blowers, aluminium cans, barbeque starter, charcoal briquettes, goods manufactured in polluting countries, dumb light bulbs, and the list goes on and on until the mind boggles.

Half the world is eating yellow snow, while the other half lives in air-conditioned comfort, and the environment gangs are poised to rake in billions of dollars to keep the status quo by creating wind farms, when all that's needed is to stop the air-conditioning of entire desert cities. If people want to live in temperate zones, so be it, but to want their every breath cooled is unnatural and a waste of resources. According to Sue Roaf, a professor and expert in environmental architecture, large hotels in Las Vegas use 400,000 megawatts of electricity per year at a cost of $40 million and produce 145 million metric tons of carbon dioxide per annum.

Worse is building ugly wind farms in Canada to support this gluttonous consumption. A better alternative would be to get off the North American power grid and keep our own house. That will never happen, because Canada makes big bucks selling the U.S. power they don't need but use anyway to cool places where nobody should be and only are because a few people and governments are raking in big bucks. Sounds autocratic, especially all those Vegas hotels, which probably produce more carbon dioxide per annum than all the cars in Canada.

But there's nothing to do about it, since the Americans will just point fingers and tell us we're using power to heat cold places where we shouldn't be living. Makes a person think about overpopulation—if there were not so many of us, Canadians could all move south and just come home to get stuff. But hey, we're doing that already. Figures from the U.S. National Association of Realtors indicate that 11 percent of all foreign buyers of homes in the United States in 2007 were Canadians, and there must be must be an equal number buying in other countries. That's a lot of Canadians with somewhere to go if our weather turns weird and we get another year without summer. Or maybe they simply want to run away, because being nagged to turn off the lights by wealthy, retired scientists can become tiring, especially when the power saved is being sold to keep hot places cold and a few folks rolling in dough.

I jumped at the chance to write this book. The weather and I go way back, and it's had me dodging lightning bolts like a cartoon character, trapped in blizzards, fogs, hurricanes, and made hanging around strange airports a kind of purgatory. But I still love it; because not only is weather the voice, it's also the personality of our planet, sometimes pleasant, often nasty, but never boring. Is it getting weird? I hope you will have made some conclusions and maybe think, well, yeah, it is, but it's always been that way. People are born, live and die—but weather is forever and offers change to every generation. To a young child, a fresh snowfall is anticipatory bliss, hail is magic, and dust devils are just about the neatest thing around. And then the child grows up, and somehow the weather is different: snow makes it hard to drive, the walk needs shovelling, hail ruins the garden, and dust devils don't rate a second look.

But there's a cure for that. Go and see the diamond dust, the fire rainbows, the northern lights, and all the other atmospheric treats, and rediscover your anticipatory childhood.

NOTES ON SOURCES

Bahr, Robert. *The Blizzard*. Toronto: Prentice-Hall, 1980.

Brown, Robert D., and Terry Gillespie. *Microclimatic Landscape Design*. New York and Toronto: John Wiley & Sons, Inc., 1995.

Couture, Pauline. *ICE*. Toronto: McArthur, 2004.

Dennis, Jerry. *It's Raining Frogs and Fishes*. New York: Harper Collins, 1992.

Lee, Albert. *Weather Wisdom*. New York: Congdon & Weed, 1976.

Lindop, Laurie. *Chasing Tornadoes*. Brookfield, Connecticut: Twenty-First Century Books, 2003.

Roaf, Sue, David Crichton, and Fergus Nico. *Adapting Buildings and Cities for Climate Change*. Amsterdam: Elsevier, 2004.

Rossi, Erno. *White Death: The Blizzard of '77*. Port Colborne, Ontario: 77 Pub, 1978.

Wolfe, S.A. "Impact of increased aridity on sand dune activity in the Canadian Prairies." *Journal of Arid Environments*. Vol. 36, 421–32. Amsterdam: Elsevier, 1997.

Online Sources

Canadian Direct Insurance; www.canadiandirect.com

The Canadian Encyclopedia; www.thecanadianencyclopedia.com

John Coleman; www.kusi.com/weather/colemanscorner/13681217.html

HighBeam Research; www.highbeam.com

Hudson's Bay Company Archives; www.gov.mb.ca

Manitoba Historical Society; www.mhs.mb.ca

Natural Resources Canada; www.nrcan.gc.ca

Nordlys Northern Lights; www.northern-lights.no

Science Daily; www.sciencedaily.com

U.S. National Weather Service; www.srh.weather.gov

The Weather Doctor; www.islandnet.com/~see/weather/doctor.htm

Wikipedia; www.wikipedia.org

Wings Magazine, Canada's Aviation Resource Centre; www.wingsmagazine.com

ABOUT THE ILLUSTRATORS

Peter Tyler

Peter is a recent graduate of the Vancouver Film School's Visual Art and Design and Classical animation programs. Though his ultimate passion is in filmmaking, he is also intent on developing his draftsmanship and storytelling, with the aim of using those skills in future filmic misadventures.

Roger Garcia

Roger Garcia is a self-taught artist with some formal training who specializes in cartooning and illustration. He is an immigrant from El Salvador, and during the last few years, his work has been primarily cartoons and editorial illustrations in pen and ink. Recently he has started painting once more. His work can be seen in newspapers, magazines, promo material and on www.rogergarcia.ca.

Patrick Hénaff

Born in France, Patrick Hénaff is mostly self-taught. He is a versatile artist who has explored a variety of media under many different influences. He now uses primarily pen and ink to draw and then processes the images on computer. He is particularly interested in the narrative power of pictures.

Roly Wood

Roly has worked in Toronto as a freelance illustrator, and was also employed in the graphic design department of a landscape architecture firm. In 2004 he wrote and illustrated a historical comic book set in Lang Pioneer Village near Peterborough, Ontario. To see more of Roly's work, visit www.rolywood.com.

ABOUT THE AUTHOR

A.H. Jackson

Born in Simcoe, Ontario, to a family of food processors, A.H. Jackson has always been fascinated by the skies above. A certified pilot, he flew his first plane at 14 and left home at 17 to continue his atmospheric exploration. Jackson believes that, in the twine of life, two special genes are unique to humankind—hope and humour—and thinks we should all turn to the funny side of life in the face of adversity. He must have quite the sense of humour then, because he's been struck by lightning five times!

Alan has co-authored a mystery—*Pretty Maids all in a Row*—and has several adventure books for young adults in the wings. He is presently working on another project for Blue Bike Books—*Weird Ontario Weather*.